THE END OF RACE POLITICS

THE END OF
RACE POLITICS

Arguments for a
Colorblind America

COLEMAN HUGHES

THESIS

Thesis
An imprint of Penguin Random House LLC
penguinrandomhouse.com

Graphs on pages 92 and 96 used with permission of Gallup, Inc.

LIBRARY OF CONGRESS CATALOGING-IN-PUBLICATION DATA
Names: Hughes, Coleman, author.
Title: The end of race politics: arguments for a colorblind America, Coleman Hughes.
Description: New York: Thesis, 2024. | Includes bibliographical references and index.
Identifiers: LCCN 2023030294 (print) | LCCN 2023030295 (ebook) |
ISBN 9780593332450 (hardcover) | ISBN 9780593332467 (ebook)
Subjects: LCSH: Race—United States. | United States—Race relations, |
Post-racialism—United States. | United States—Social policy—History—21st century.
Classification: LCC HT1561 .H84 2024 (print) | LCC HT1561 (ebook) |
DDC 305.800973—dc23/eng/20231117
LC record available at https://lccn.loc.gov/2023030294
LC ebook record available at https://lccn.loc.gov/2023030295

Printed in the United States of America
1st Printing

Book design by Alissa Rose Theodor

For Santa Cruz Hughes,
whose light was extinguished far too soon.

CONTENTS

———

INTRODUCTION

———

Why Write about Race?

I've always found race boring. Sure, it can be good source material for jokes at a comedy club. But in most real-life situations, a person's race tells you next to nothing about them. It doesn't tell whether they're kind or selfish, whether their opinions are right or wrong, whether they'll become your best friend or your worst enemy. Of all the qualities you could list about somebody—their personality, beliefs, sense of humor, and so forth—their race is just about the least interesting you could name.

So if I find race to be a meaningless trait, why write a whole book about it? The answer is simple: I didn't choose the topic of race; it chose me.

I am what you would call "half-black, half-Hispanic," or, simply, "black" (we will see in chapter one how these categories change depending on time and place). For most of my young life, I rarely thought about my racial identity. I had black friends, white friends, Asian friends, Hispanic friends, and mixed-race friends. But I didn't think of them as "black," "white," "Hispanic," and "mixed race." I thought of them as Rodney, Stephen, Javier, and Jordan.

For the most part, the people I grew up around seemed to share my lack of interest in race. They agreed with Martin Luther King Jr.'s famous dictum about the content of one's character trumping the color of one's skin—even if collective overuse had already made it a cliché. On the rare occasion that some petty person did try to use race as a weapon—to bully someone, for instance—the dominant value system would come down on them like a tornado. They would be ostracized and punished. Where I grew up in Montclair, New Jersey, racists existed, but they were the exceedingly rare exceptions that proved the overwhelming rule.

Montclair's well-loved public schools were my home until the sixth grade, when I enrolled at a fancy private school several towns away. Though the education I received at this new school was undoubtedly better, the social transition was awkward. The main locus of this awkwardness was my large, voluminous afro.

In my hometown public school, where around one in three students were black, afros were commonplace. Kids of every race were used to seeing them. But at Newark Academy I was a novelty. There were only four black students in an entering class of over sixty kids, and most of the nonblack students did not come from racially diverse towns like Montclair. Many of them had never known somebody with an afro. What began as an understandable curiosity about my hairstyle grew into a ubiquitous and apparently irresistible urge to touch it—usually ruining whatever preparation I had done that morning to get it looking just right.

I hoped this was just passing curiosity. But as the weeks turned into months, it became clear that the urge to touch my hair was insatiable. To make matters worse, no single person pestered me enough to be singled out. The blame was distributed among so many kids that it could not be solved by talking to any one of them—death by a thousand cuts.

Eventually I broke down. Thoroughly frustrated with my peers—and ashamed that I had let the problem grow to such proportions—I cried hot tears to my parents. I was tired of having my hair ruined by my classmates' curiosity, tired of being treated like a novelty act. I don't remember whether the problem stopped after my parents talked to the school principal. But what I do remember is that by seventh grade the afro was gone, replaced by an unassuming fade (in retrospect, a way better choice anyway).

Four years later, when I was sixteen, the higher-ups at Newark Academy offered me the chance to attend a three-day event in Houston called the People of Color Conference. I said yes, jumping at the opportunity to miss three days of class. Misleadingly, the conference was not just for people of color but for private school students of all races—hundreds of us from around the nation. Though I wouldn't have known to call it this at the time, the conference was essentially a three-day critical race theory and intersectionality workshop. It was there that I first heard terms like systemic racism, safe space, white privilege, and internalized oppression—ideas that were fringe in 2012 but would sweep through the elite universities just a few years later. Up until 2012, I had never been immersed in a subculture where my race was considered to be important. The People of Color

Conference changed that. At the conference, my blackness was not considered a neutral fact—irrelevant to my deeper qualities as a human being. My blackness was instead considered a kind of magic. My skin color was discussed as if it were a beautiful enigma at the core of my identity, a slice of God inside my soul.

The conference leaders taught us one idea that pertained directly to my unfortunate afro experience from middle school: a *microaggression*. A microaggression, I learned, was a statement or action that conveys subtle, unintentional discrimination against members of a marginalized group. Before learning this term, I had filed the afro fiasco under the heading of difficult experiences that many kids face in middle school. In fact, I recall thinking that it was not nearly as bad as the verbal abuse experienced by my white friend for being an unlucky mix of pale, skinny, nerdy, and awkward—bullying that eventually prompted him to leave the school. Nor was it anywhere close to the mocking endured by the overweight, pimply white kid whose manner of speech seemed to be permanently slurred. In truth, it wasn't even bullying. The kids touching my afro were never malicious, only curious. They never teased me or insulted me. And I easily got along with them in every other context. As annoying as their behavior was, the obvious goodwill behind their actions softened my judgment of them.

At the conference, however, I was taught to frame my experience differently. It was a microaggression. Whereas bullying can be experienced by anyone, only members of marginalized groups can experience microaggressions. My afro experience was placed on the same continuum as the violent racism I had learned about in history class. At one end of that continuum was Emmett Till and the brave civil rights protesters beaten at Selma. And on the less severe end of that same continuum was me. I had experienced a microdose of the same poison. I was taught that my victimization was special, and that made me special. Where my white friends had the wind of white supremacy at their backs, I faced a headwind. And everything I had accomplished in spite of it was that much more impressive as a result.

That was the ideology that I, along with hundreds of other students, absorbed at this three-day conference. The atmosphere, however, was less scholarly than it was spiritual. For instance, many of the students at the conference were gay and came from households that were socially conservative. For some, the conference was the first time in their entire lives that they could voice their sexuality out loud without fear of judgment. There was crying and hugging and warmth. In those ways, the energy in the room was uplifting.

But in other ways, it was suffocating. The teachers enforced a strict orthodoxy; dissent was never welcomed and was therefore rarely even attempted. You could no more challenge the doctrines being taught than you could argue that God doesn't exist from a Sunday morning church pulpit. As a kid who enjoyed debating with professors, I couldn't help but notice, and lament, the stifling conformism.

After my brief foray into the strange, race-obsessed world of the POC Conference, I returned to my life as a high school student who cared about music and philosophy, and who connected with others on the basis of shared interests rather than race. I never imagined that the subculture I encountered in Houston would appear in my life again.

Then I enrolled at Columbia University.

In the three years since I'd attended the conference, the ideas I encountered there had spread to elite high schools and universities throughout the nation. During orientation week at Columbia, we were asked to divide ourselves up by race and discuss how we either participated in, or suffered from, systemic oppression. I huddled with the black kids in one corner of the room, and watched as the white kids, Hispanic kids, and Asian kids awkwardly shuffled to their respective corners.

Whatever the intent of this ice-breaking exercise, the effect was that I felt acutely aware of my blackness. And that awareness ironically made me feel less connected to the people around me, not more. I worried that rather than approach me as a blank slate, these students would approach me as a black man, and, by implication, a victim.

In four years at Columbia, hardly a week passed without a race-themed controversy. In the school newspaper, students would say they experienced white supremacy "every day" on campus. A professor of mine once told our class that "all people of color were by definition victims of oppression," even as my daily experience as a black person directly contradicted that claim. It felt as if I was dropped into a simulation where the Real Racism dial was set close to zero, but the Concern About Racism dial was set to ten. Though I found the topic of race to be boring in and of itself, the surrounding culture was obsessed with it—and was hell-bent on dragging me in.

Eventually, I became curious. Why were white students and professors confessing their inner racism unprompted? Why were black students in one of the most progressive, non-racist environments on Earth claiming to experience racism every day? And why were so many otherwise reasonable people pretending to believe them? Why did these kids sound more pessimistic about the state of American race relations than my grandparents (who lived through segregation) do?

The more I asked these questions, the more I became convinced that the new race obsession that brands itself "anti-racist" is in fact the opposite. It is racist, destructive, and contrary to the spirit of the civil rights movement. Taken to their logical endpoints, the ideas I encountered first at the POC Conference and then at Columbia pave the way toward a social and political hellscape where skin color—a meaningless trait—is given supreme importance.

If these ideas were confined to high school conferences and Ivy League universities, one could make the case that they are not worth worrying about. But they have infected all of our key institutions: government, education, and media. Some of our most celebrated and sought-after public intellectuals routinely espouse ideas so extreme that the public has been desensitized to them.

Consider the ideas of Robin DiAngelo, best-selling author of *White Fragility*. DiAngelo argues that white Americans, simply by virtue of being raised in America, are all racist. There is no cure for this racism, she argues, but there is a treatment: adopting what I call "DiAngelo etiquette." DiAngelo etiquette outlines a strict set of rules that white people should adopt when speaking to black people about race: don't argue, don't push back, don't remain silent, and don't withdraw. By process of elimination, the only option left is to vocally agree with whatever is said—hardly the basis of a healthy relationship between equals.

Or consider the following proposal from MacArthur Genius and best-selling author Ibram X. Kendi. In an article for *Politico*, Kendi proposed that we pass a constitutional amendment that establishes and permanently funds a Department of Anti-Racism (DOA) staffed by racism "experts." According to Kendi, these experts would be tasked with blocking any local, state, or federal law from going into effect if it determines that the law would have a racist impact. They would also be tasked with defining "racist ideas" and disciplining public figures who express them. To add a cherry on top of this totalitarian cake, the experts at the DOA could not be hired or fired by any politician, including the president.

Though we are unlikely to see the DOA become a reality anytime soon, Kendi's other ideas are rapidly becoming accepted. Since the civil rights movement, a majority of Americans have agreed that discriminating against somebody because of their race is morally unacceptable. Kendi disagrees. He believes that certain kinds of racial discrimination are good and necessary:

> The only remedy to racist discrimination is antiracist discrimination. The only remedy to past discrimination is present discrimination. The only remedy to present discrimination is future discrimination.

The lesson of the centuries-long history of racism against black Americans—from slavery, convict leasing, and lynching to separate but equal and redlining—is that racial discrimination tends to create an enormous amount of justified resentment in the population discriminated against. Instead of learning that lesson, many people want to implement new regimes of discrimination against new groups of people. I call these "Kendi laws," and as we will see in chapter three, they have already been implemented at the highest levels of government.

In this book, I will argue that colorblindness is the wisest principle by which to govern our fragile experiment in multi-ethnic democracy. My hope is that this book will help people think more clearly about the long-run consequences of race thinking and race-based policy, restore our faith in the guiding principle of colorblindness, and pave a constructive path forward in our national conversation on race.

THE END OF RACE POLITICS

1

Race, Anti-racism, and Neoracism

For most of my life, I saw my mother as neither black nor white. Her Puerto Rican father was darker-skinned than me and her Puerto Rican mother was as light-skinned as any white American I knew. My mother emerged a perfect blend of the two: a light-brown hue that suggested neither blackness nor whiteness—at least not to my mind. Nor did I view her as "Hispanic," a word she hated due to its association with Spanish conquest, or even as "Latina"—though she would certainly have checked that box on a census.

She would sometimes describe herself as "of color." But whenever she really cared to show her identity, she would say she was Puerto Rican, and more specifically *Nuyorican*—a person who grew up in one of the Puerto Rican enclaves of New York City. Just as important, she would say that she was from the Bronx, and more specifically the *South* Bronx. Had you asked me what "race" my mother belonged to as a child or adolescent, that would have been my long-winded answer: she was a Puerto

Rican/NewYorican from the South Bronx. The words "black" and "white" would not have even occurred to me.

My mother died of cancer when I was eighteen. In the wake of her passing, I took every opportunity to talk about her with anyone who remembered her. I was surprised one time to hear a friend of mine describe her simply as "a black woman." "You saw my mom as black?" I asked him. "Well, sure. She was, wasn't she?" I had never considered that the outside world might have perceived her differently. In the case of my friend, I wrote this off as a misperception born of not knowing her very well.

So it came as an even greater shock when my father, who knew her as well as anyone, agreed with my friend. "Your mother was a black woman," he told me years after she died. I was shocked. I had never seen her as black and I never heard her describe herself that way. I had seen her as an immigrant outside the American black-white binary. Yet many people saw her simply as a light-skinned black American woman.

I am tempted to insist that my memory of her identity is accurate, and that others' perceptions of her are simply mistaken. But what would it even mean for their perceptions to be "mistaken"? What does it mean to belong to one race or another? Is it a matter of scientific fact, self-identification, perception by others, cultural background, or arbitrary social convention?

WHAT IS RACE?

I've been using the word "race" without defining it. Indeed, most of us use it all the time without thinking about what it is. Yet we are constantly arguing about it. For a moment, forget that you ever learned the word "race." Let's begin at the most basic level.

The Concept of Race

We humans use concepts to make sense of the world. Some concepts are natural and others are socially constructed.

In science, for instance, our goal is to describe nature. So we develop concepts and categories that map onto nature as closely as possible, such as the concept of a tree or the concept of mass in physics. These are natural concepts—concepts that map onto nature with great precision. If for some reason these concepts disappeared from our minds, we'd be forced by logic and our senses to reinvent them in much the same way. Natural concepts carve reality at the joints.

Other times, our goal is not to describe nature but to create a desirable outcome in society. For example, if we're trying to count time, we may invent the concept of a week—a unit of time that's equal to the sun rising and setting seven times—so that everyone can be on the same page about when to do things.

The seven-day week doesn't exist in nature. We could've decided that a week equals six days or eight days. Or we could have no weeks at all—counting time only by days. We invented the concept of a week to achieve an important goal: ease of coordination with others. And if our minds were suddenly wiped clean of the concept of a week, we might not reinvent it in exactly the same way. This concept, in other words, is a social construct.

The concept of race falls into a third category. It's neither completely natural nor completely socially constructed. It's a social construct *inspired by* a natural phenomenon.

To take a simple example, consider the concept of a month. Months don't exist in nature; they don't track anything in the natural world. Nothing in the cosmos begins when February does or ends when March does. We could just as easily end March a day later and give April an extra day. Or we could get rid of March altogether and distribute its days among the remaining eleven months.

On the other hand, months are clearly inspired by something that does exist in nature: the lunar cycle. It is no accident that months are similar in length to the lunar cycle, which averages 29.5 days. (The words "moon" and "month" even derive from the same root.) So what is a month? It's not a natural phenomenon because it doesn't track anything in the natural world with precision. Therefore, it must be a social construct. Yet unlike most social constructs, it owes its very existence and basic characteristics to a natural phenomenon. It is thus a kind of hybrid: a social construct inspired by a natural phenomenon.

The concept of race is similar to the concept of a month. It too is a social construct inspired by a natural phenomenon. What natural phenomenon is the concept of race inspired by?

Tens of thousands of years ago, several large populations of humans migrated out of Africa, where all humans first evolved (Africans, of course, remained in Africa). Once out of Africa, these populations remained isolated from one another—separated by mountains, oceans, or great distances. As a result of living and reproducing in unique environments for tens of thousands of years, each group's gene pool evolved in response to the unique selection pressures of its environment.

The legacy of these genetic differences is still visible and measurable today. Although each of us is genetically unique (barring identical twins), each of us also belongs to clusters of similar genomes whose similarity stems from the major out-of-Africa migrations that occurred tens of thousands of years ago. These clusters are not sharply separated from one another. They overlap a great deal, and therefore the boundaries between them are blurry. Using standard statistical tools, the strength of these genome clusters can be measured. The visible correlates of these genetically similar clusters are the underlying natural phenomena that inspired the concept of race. (See Appendix A for more details.)

But as with the concept of a month, the social construct has been untethered from the natural phenomenon that inspired it. If tomorrow astronomers discovered that the lunar cycle was really 35 days instead of 29.5, that discovery would have no bearing at all on the length of a calendar month. Likewise, whatever population geneticists discover about the clustering of similar genomes—for instance, if they were to discover something that completely upends our current understanding of population genetics—that would have no bearing on the concept of race that we use socially and in public policy. The social construct of race has flown the perch of the natural phenomenon that inspired it.

The Arbitrariness of Race

As we will see in chapter three, many of today's anti-racists are adamant on implementing race-based policies throughout every sector of society. One problem with this approach is that it's impossible to draw neat lines between races. And the lines that we end up drawing are not based on science nor reason but on a variety of absurd factors. President Barack Obama is the son of a white mother and a black father, so we categorize Obama as black. But why? His parentage is equal parts "black" and "white," so on what basis do we categorize him as black rather than white or mixed? The answer, it seems, is that American culture still observes the old "one-drop rule"—whereby anyone with one drop of "black blood" is considered fully black. In other words, we choose to delineate race using an arbitrary rule that was originally developed to uphold racial apartheid.

Similarly, our society decided how to answer the question "Who is Asian?" during the Chinese Exclusion Act—a racist law that existed to define a group of people to exclude. Decades later, the Eisenhower administration needed to come up with race categories to implement its policies and decided on a perfunctory list. But it was the Carter administration that finally decided on the canonical list of five categories we use today: Black, Hispanic, White, Asian/Pacific Islander, Native American/Alaska Native.

Population geneticists were not consulted to help create these categories (nor could they have spoken with real authority prior to the sequencing of the genome). These categories were created based upon a vague mix of intuitions about racial difference and political lobbyists attempting to sway the categorization in one direction or another. To qualify for certain government programs, for instance, someone needs to have one-fourth Native American ancestry. Why one-fourth? Why not one-half? Why not one-eighth? Why not one-sixteenth? The answer is that administering social programs requires drawing sharp lines that don't exist in nature, so they simply decided to draw it at the one-fourth mark.

The Asian American category includes people from India and Pakistan but not from Afghanistan. Again, the reason has nothing to do with science and everything to do with the race-based social policy that could not be administered without a crisp definition of who fits into which race.

Think likewise of the Hispanic category. "Hispanic" describes anyone with ancestry from a Spanish-speaking country, but sometimes it's treated as a race, other times as an ethnicity. You can be categorized as either black Hispanic or white Hispanic, but for many practical purposes (for college admissions, say) either designation qualifies as a preferred racial category. In some cases, Spanish Europeans and Indigenous Peruvians are considered in the same category, because they're both from Spanish-speaking nations. Yet Brazilians are also sometimes counted as Hispanic. It is also worth noting that unlike "black" and "white," "Hispanic" and "Asian" are not terms that belonged to the self-concept of the people in those categories when they were created. Few Hispanic people understood themselves to be "Hispanic" when the term was first widely used in the 1970s. A recent survey found that only 30 percent of "Asian Americans" thought of themselves as "Asian." Most thought of themselves as belonging to a specific ethnic group, such as "Korean" or "Pakistani."

David E. Bernstein describes a case that illustrates the arbitrariness of using race categories to distribute social benefits:

Christine Combs and Steve Lynn applied to the Small Business Administration (SBA) to have their respective businesses certified as Hispanic-owned and therefore eligible for minority business enterprise preferences. Combs's maternal grandparents were born in Spain, she grew up in a bilingual family, was fluent in Spanish, and acted as an interpreter for Mexican and Spanish customers. Lynn's sole claim to Hispanic status was that he was a Sephardic Jew whose ancestors had fled Spain centuries earlier.

The SBA ultimately decided that Lynn qualified as Hispanic, but Combs did not. Combs's SBA hearing officer declared that Combs could not claim Hispanic status . . . because she presented no evidence that she had faced discrimination because she is Hispanic. The officer noted that neither Combs's maiden name nor her married name was recognizably Spanish, and her blond hair and blue eyes did not give her a noticeably Hispanic appearance. On appeal, a judge found that the hearing officer had "reason to question Ms. Combs' status as a Hispanic." The judge therefore upheld the denial of Combs's petition.

An SBA hearing officer also initially denied Lynn's claim to Hispanic status because Lynn had not shown that he had been discriminated against as a Hispanic. But when Lynn appealed, the judge noted that the underlying law defined Hispanic as including anyone of Spanish origin or culture, which includes Sephardic Jews. The judge concluded that once Lynn showed that he had Spanish ancestry, the hearing officer should not have required him to also provide evi-

dence that he had faced discrimination because of that ancestry.

Another example of the arbitrariness of race categories comes
from Kao Lee Yang, a doctoral student in neuroscience at the
University of Wisconsin-Madison. She is Hmong, a group of people indigenous to Southeast Asia. The Hmong people are an Asian
ethnic group that is, on average, low-income and very underrepresented in American higher education. Because of this, her university nominated her to apply for a fellowship aimed at supporting
underrepresented groups in science. But her nomination was re-
jected on the grounds that she was not, in fact, underrepresented.
For them she was not categorized as Hmong specifically but in the
more generic "Asian" category—a group that is overrepresented in
American higher education.

The Asian category comprises an extremely broad range of
people—so broad that the Pew Research Center found wider income inequality within that category than within any other racial group: the top-earning Asians earn 10.7 times as much as the
lowest-earning Asians. By comparison, the top-earning blacks
earn 9.8 times as much as the lowest-earning blacks, and the top-
earning whites and Hispanics earn 7.8 times as much as the
lowest-earning whites and Hispanics. Disparities in income levels among Asians are matched by disparities in education levels.
In 2015, 72 percent of Indians over 25 had at least a bachelor's
degree. Yet only 9 percent of Bhutanese did.

All of the foregoing examples illustrate that the race categories we've created are arbitrary—not only with respect to science

but also with respect to the social policy objectives they are used for. Yet despite that arbitrariness, these categories have a huge impact on people's lives. Whether you're eligible for a scholarship, admission to a prestigious school, government funding to help your small business, or a variety of other societal benefits depends on whether you land on one side or the other of a nonsensical racial line. These racial distinctions are bound to unfairly advantage or disadvantage certain people. They constitute a textbook case of injustice.

The arbitrariness of race is not a fixable problem. It's built into the very act of classifying people by race. In apartheid South Africa, government officials would run a pencil through people's hair to determine their race. If the pencil went through, you were legally white. If it didn't, you were legally colored. However more enlightened we believe ourselves to be (and we are in many ways), our methods of classifying people by race are equally absurd. We just can't see it because we take our conventions for granted. We cringe when we hear old recordings of people describe Asians as "yellow" and Native Americans as "red," then we proceed to talk about "black," "brown," and "white" people with a straight face—as if the generations past were simpletons with respect to racial classification, but we are far superior.

A critic might agree with this point, but draw the conclusion that we need better categories. The problem isn't with racial classification in general, they might say, the problem is with the specific race categories we've chosen to adopt. The solution is to adopt better categories—to draw better lines—not to jettison racial classification altogether.

This objection fails to understand the depth of the problem. Even if it were possible to create rational racial categories (which it isn't), those categories still would not map onto the things that we should really care about: namely addressing poverty, disadvantage, and disparities of luck.

In the end, it's impossible to avoid the unfair policies that result from using arbitrary racial distinctions to dole out social advantages or disadvantages. The way to avoid this kind of unfairness isn't to come up with different race categories; it's to get out of the business of racial classification altogether.

What's Better Than Race?

We often use race as a proxy for other things we care about. For example, when lawmakers discuss policies aimed at helping the disadvantaged, they'll use race as a proxy for disadvantage. They will use expressions like "blacks, Hispanics, and other disadvantaged groups" to refer to the people their policies are aimed at helping.

But whether we are talking about current disadvantages (what is sometimes called "privilege") or historical disadvantages, racial identity is a bad proxy. If all whites were advantaged, it would make sense for practical purposes to equate whiteness with advantage. If all blacks were impoverished, then it would make sense for practical purposes to equate blackness with poverty. But racialized generalizations like these don't work. There's no version of "white people are X" or "black people are Y" that provides an accurate rule of thumb for addressing issues like poverty or historical injustice. When it comes to policies that try to correct for disparities of luck, we should use more accurate proxies.

Imagine that we picked one hundred Americans at random. Our task is to line them up from "least privileged" to "most privileged" so that we can use public policy to prioritize the least advantaged among them. Because there is no direct measure of privilege, we would have to choose a proxy. My claim is that lining everyone up by socioeconomic status—income, wealth, or some combination measure—would get us closer to our goal than lining them up by racial identity would. That is what I mean when I say that income is a better proxy for disadvantage than race.

Nor is race a good proxy for historical victimhood. One in five black Americans is either a first- or second-generation immigrant, which means they have no ancestral connection to American slavery. And that number is projected to grow substantially in the next few decades. This means that policies aimed at addressing the descendants of American slaves, for instance, cannot use black identity as a simple proxy for historical victimhood. When we have more accurate proxies, we should ditch race and use those better proxies instead.

Someone might object, "Coleman, I agree that an individual's income/wealth is a more accurate proxy for disadvantage than his race, but doesn't race play a role as well? If I were to compare two people who grew up with the same level of income, on average, the black person will have experienced more racial discrimination than the white person, right? So rather than never using race in public policy, why not use it as a kind of tiebreaker, once the more important variables such as income have already been taken into account?"

I will have more to say about this argument in chapters five and six, but for now I'll say this: The status quo in American public policy for the past several decades has been to use race as the *main* proxy for disadvantage. If you favor using race only as a tiebreaker once better proxies have been taken into account, then you are in favor of a vast overhaul of the status quo in the direction that I am arguing for—even if you do not follow me all the way to my conclusion.

The idea that race should be removed from public policy isn't new, as we will see in chapter two. Among other things it was the long-held position of the NAACP. The organization's general counsel, Robert L. Carter, stated the point in the early 1960s: "If we are prepared to accept the basic postulate of our society— that race or color is an irrelevance—then contentions that race and color statistics are of social science value become sheer sophistical rationalizations."

On one level, the case against race-based policy is similar to the case against laws restricting speech. Rather than allowing politicians and judges wide discretion in determining what kinds of speech laws are constitutional, the First Amendment applies an incredibly high and specific bar for prohibiting speech. The logic behind this high bar is that politicians and judges cannot be trusted to wield this power. It is too tempting to use, and too often used for ill.

The same skepticism of state power underlies the case against race-based government policy. The history of America—from slavery to Jim Crow through today's neoracist policies that I'll describe in chapter three—gives no indication that politicians and judges can be trusted to apply the concept of race wisely. Yet in spite of this consistently shameful record, many people seem to believe that lurking just around the corner is the moment when we will finally elect and appoint public officials who will implement only the good race-based policies and never the bad ones—public officials with excellent judgment on issues of race. This is dangerous wishful thinking. As with speech, it would be wiser to take the power to racially discriminate out of their hands altogether. As we'll see in chapter two, this is what many of our most celebrated activists have tried to do throughout history.

There are alternative concepts, such as socioeconomic status, that correspond more closely to the kinds of things we care about addressing as a society and that are better at helping us achieve our desired social ends. We need to start using those concepts instead of race to shape our public policy.

ANTI-RACISM

As I stand here and look out upon the thousands of Negro faces, and the thousands of white faces, intermingled like the waters of a river, I see only one face—the face of the future.
—DR. MARTIN LUTHER KING JR.

In envisioning a future for America, I imagine a country where citizens live securely and exercise their freedom to seek happiness. A country devoid of second-class citizens, where democracy thrives and politicians remain answerable to the people they represent. This nation would provide each child with an education that challenges them, equipping them with the skills required to become responsible adults.

I envision a country that offers each child a rigorous education, equipping them with the necessary skills to mature into responsible adults. This America would boast a resilient economy, with stable growth, infrequent recessions, and abundant job opportunities. It would be a place that provides comprehensive health care for its citizens and dedicates resources to help those who cannot support themselves.

In such an America, people would feel at ease in their neighborhoods, free from the threat of stalking or harassment or violence. This nation would be a global leader in technological advancement, while ensuring that technology serves the people, not the other way around. It would be a diverse society where individuals hold varying beliefs but are united in their dedication to addressing disputes through dialogue, not violence. People would be free to engage in candid, open conversations without the fear of being marginalized or "canceled."

The dream I just laid out references many important concepts: health, wealth, and safety, to name a few. One concept it did not mention is race. Nor did it mention any related concepts like skin color or ancestry. These omissions are intentional. I think race is irrelevant to the things we care most about in life, and dividing people by race is an obstacle to realizing this dream. In my ideal future, the people of this country would be so busy pursuing the things that really matter that we might go weeks or months at a time without ever thinking about the concept of race.

The Dream

I call it "my dream," but I'm not the first to have had it. It was also the dream of Dr. Martin Luther King Jr.—the one he shared with the nation on the steps of the Lincoln Memorial:

> I have a dream that my four little children will one day live in a nation where they will not be judged by the color of their skin but by the content of their character. I have a *dream* today!
>
> I have a dream that one day, down in Alabama, with its vicious racists, with its governor having his lips dripping with the words of interposition and nullification, one day right there in Alabama little black boys and black girls will be able to join hands with little white boys and white girls as sisters and brothers. I have a *dream* today!

King wasn't the first to have this dream either. His dream was rooted in the American dream—a dream about our common humanity and our common striving for the good life. It's a dream that recognizes that human well-being has nothing essential to do with skin color, ancestry, or the other traits people have used throughout history to divide societies and to invite hatred, fear, and needless suffering into their lives.

It's a dream that true anti-racists throughout our nation's history have struggled to make a reality—the dream of Frederick

Douglass, of Henry Highland Garnet, of Wendell Phillips, and other famous abolitionists; the dream of Zora Neale Hurston, of A. Philip Randolph, and Bayard Rustin—heroic opponents of race-based policies and leaders of the civil rights movement.

It's also a dream that has had many enemies throughout American history and that continues to have many enemies today—enemies who think that race matters in some deep way to who we are and how we ought to live.

We can all agree that people often choose to make race matter in a particular situation. For instance, if a cop pulls me over because of my race, or an employer denies me a promotion because of my race, they've chosen to make race matter in that particular situation.

What sets enemies of the dream apart is their insistence that race matters *regardless of circumstance*—their insistence that race matters for reasons that go beyond our individual choices, beliefs, and values. Enemies of the dream believe that there are deep and enduring reasons to divide humanity into races, though they disagree on what those reasons are. Old-school race supremacists, for instance, believe that race matters for biological or theological reasons: that white people are entitled to a superior position in society because of better genetics (see, for example, Madison Grant's infamous book *The Passing of the Great Race*) or that black people are superior because God ordained it so (see, for example, Elijah Muhammad's *Message to the Blackman in America*, a foundational text in the Nation of Islam).

But as old-school race supremacy has lost influence, a new school of racism has risen to take its place. I call it *neoracism*. Neoracists agree that race matters deeply and inherently, but not because of genetics or divine decree. Instead, they believe race matters for societal and historical reasons: that discrimination in favor of non-whites is justified on account of the hardships they endure—and hardships their ancestors endured—at the hands of whites.

Old-school race supremacists and modern-day neoracists may seem very different from one another (and they are in many respects), but they agree that race matters in a deep and enduring way. They agree that viewing ourselves and others through the lens of race is central to improving our society, our relationships, and even our private lives.

The dream, by contrast, rejects racist thinking of every kind: old-school, new-school, anti-black, anti-white, and so forth. It embraces a different philosophy of race—the same philosophy that motivated the civil rights movement and much of the abolitionist movement. It's the philosophy that we should treat people—both in our private lives and in our public policy—without regard to race. Many anti-racists have a name for this philosophy. We call it "colorblindness."

The Colorblind Principle

Any explanation of colorblindness should begin by explaining what it isn't.

We all see race. We can't help it. What's more, race can influence how we're treated and how we treat others. We are all capable of racial bias. In that sense, no one is truly colorblind. Even people who are literally colorblind—because their eyes lack the right number of cones—still effortlessly distinguish between people of different races.

But to interpret the expression "colorblind" so literally is to misunderstand the philosophy of colorblindness that I seek to defend. Rather, "colorblind" is an expression like "warmhearted": it uses a physical metaphor to reference an abstract idea. To describe a person as warmhearted is not to say something about the temperature of their heart but about the kindness of their spirit. Similarly, to advocate colorblindness is not to pretend you don't notice race. To advocate colorblindness is to endorse an ethical principle:

The colorblind principle: we should treat people without regard to race, both in our public policy and in our private lives.

That is the principle that I have in mind when I talk about colorblindness in this book.

Confusion surrounding the colorblind principle is partly the fault of its advocates. Often, for instance, they use phrases like "I don't see color" as a way of expressing their commitment to colorblindness. But phrases like that are virtually guaranteed to produce the sort of confusion I've just described. (See Appendix B for more detail on the terminology I use in this book.)

Defenders of colorblindness would do themselves a favor by eliminating phrases like "I don't see color" from their vocabularies and instead using phrases like "I try to treat people without regard to race." The aim of colorblindness isn't to avoid noticing race. For most of us, that's impossible. The aim of colorblindness is to consciously disregard race as a reason to treat individuals differently and as a category on which to base public policy.

NEORACISM

The modern neoracist movement defines itself in opposition to the colorblind principle. Here, for instance, is an example of racial stereotyping from a neoracist, the author Robin DiAngelo:

> I strive to be "less white." To be less white is to be less racially oppressive. This requires me to be more racially aware, to be better educated about racism, and to continually challenge racial certitude and arrogance. To be less white is to be open to, interested in, and compassionate toward the racial realities of people of color.

DiAngelo's statements operate using a racial stereotype. They imply that being white is tantamount to being arrogant and ignorant about race, to feeling guilty and defensive about it, to being closed-minded, uninterested in and uncompassionate toward the struggles of non-white people, to engaging in racist patterns of social interaction.

DiAngelo doesn't describe particular individuals. She doesn't accuse Fred of acting defensively or Ginger of believing she can't be friends with black people. DiAngelo instead describes a general category—whiteness—that encompasses a range of characteristic beliefs, actions, and attitudes. That's exactly what a stereotype is. It's what psychologists call a "heuristic"—a mental shortcut allowing the user to make sweeping judgments about entire groups of individuals: "All white people are X"; "All black people are Y."

The problem with racial stereotypes is not that they're never true. In fact, stereotypes often do reflect truths about *average* differences between groups of people. This is why racial humor so often rings true, even to the group being caricatured. The real problem with stereotypes is that they reduce unique individuals to the average characteristics of their group, provoking justified anger and resentment. I view the anger experienced in these moments as akin to road rage: counterproductive, perhaps, but totally understandable. Being stereotyped can feel like being accused of a crime that you know you didn't commit.

What's true of DiAngelo is true of other neoracists. Ta-Nehisi Coates, for instance, claims that Kanye West is a champion of "White freedom," which he describes as follows:

> Freedom without consequence, freedom without criticism, freedom to be proud and ignorant; freedom to profit off a people in one moment and abandon them in the next; a Stand Your Ground freedom, freedom without responsibility, without hard memory; a Monticello without slavery, a Confederate freedom, the freedom of John C. Calhoun . . . a conqueror's freedom, freedom of the strong built on antipathy or indifference to the weak, the freedom of rape buttons, pussy grabbers, and *fuck you anyway, bitch*; freedom of oil and invisible

wars, the freedom of suburbs drawn with red lines, the white freedom of Calabasas.

Neoracists have even built political support into the concept of race. Back when he was campaigning, President Joe Biden said, "If you have a problem deciding whether you're for me or Trump, then you ain't black."

What's so insidious about the new form of racism that's emerged in American society—what I call "neoracism"—is that it invokes the names of people like Martin Luther King Jr. and Frederick Douglass while betraying their deepest convictions. It's like a company that keeps the same label on the packaging while completely changing the product inside.

Neoracism insists that sharp racial classifications are a necessary part of a just society. But they don't use these categories as mere descriptors. They use terms like "blackness" and "whiteness" to encompass far more than descriptions of skin color and ancestry. They use those terms to encompass all kinds of stereotypes—stereotypes about thoughts, attitudes, beliefs, habits, and character.

The civil rights movement fought against all kinds of racial stereotyping. It fought against any kind of race thinking that discouraged us from seeing other people as individual human beings—any kind of thinking that encouraged us to see people instead as undifferentiated representatives of a collective mass: the white, the black.

Civil rights leaders saw race thinking as dehumanizing—a way of seeing people that opposed our common humanity and the importance of individual character. Think again of Dr. King:

The important thing about man is "not his specificity but his fundamentum," not the texture of his hair or the color of his skin but the quality of his soul.

Likewise, on the subject of interracial marriage, Dr. King objected to the term itself. "Properly speaking," he wrote, "races do not marry; individuals marry."

Another great anti-racist, Zora Neale Hurston, author of the classic novel *Their Eyes Were Watching God*, opposed any concept that would subordinate individuals to groups. "Races have never done anything," she wrote in her autobiography. "What seems race achievement is the work of individuals." Notions like race pride, race consciousness, and even racial solidarity, she argued, were fictions that people accepted because they appealed to base instincts.

You might think, "Coleman, you're attacking a straw man. You're mischaracterizing how neoracists view the concept of race. They don't deny that race is socially constructed, as you've suggested. On the contrary, they're very vocal about race being a social construct. Robin DiAngelo, for instance, explicitly argues that race is a social construct. Ibram X. Kendi instead argues that race is a 'power construct,' but a construct nonetheless."

This objection overlooks an important point about neoracists: though neoracists say they believe that race is a social construct, their actions point in exactly the opposite direction.

Suppose your new friend Tom tells you that he's an atheist—that he does not believe in the existence of any God, nor in the truth of any religion or Holy book. Now suppose that you slowly discovered that every other belief and value Tom has is perfectly compatible with a literalist reading of the Bible. Tom believes that the world is six thousand years old. He doesn't believe in evolution. He even refuses to wear clothing woven with two different kinds of fabric (Leviticus 19:19). When you press him on his bizarre beliefs and lifestyle choices, he insists that they have nothing to do with believing in a God, much less a Christian God. Nevertheless, you can't find any beliefs or habits he has that don't align with every jot and tittle of the King James Bible. How much stock would you place in Tom's claim to be an atheist?

Neoracists are like Tom. They say they believe that race is a social construct, but they don't act in accordance with that belief. The hallmark of believing something is a social construct is taking that social construct *less* seriously—relaxing the rules and norms surrounding it. Neoracists do just the opposite. They create and enforce strict rules and norms that govern how people of different races are supposed to interact. DiAngelo insists, for instance, that white women shouldn't cry in front of black people. Neoracists are the most likely to insist that black people can use a certain word that starts with the letter *N* but no one else can in any context. Neoracists are the most likely to insist that someone with European ancestry must not open a Mexican food restaurant. Out of everyone in Western society, neoracists (along with old-school racists) are the most fixated on enforcing the rules and norms surrounding the concept of race. They police the rules of race with a zeal that they could not possibly have if they really believed it was just a social construct.

To use another analogy: Suppose your new friend Emily tells you that she believes gender is a social construct. But slowly you discover that Emily polices the rules of gender strictly. She believes women should always wear skirts and men should wear pants, that women belong in the kitchen and men in the workplace, and so forth. No doubt, this would undermine her claim to believe that gender is a social construct. In fact, she wouldn't even have to believe in the old-fashioned rules of gender to seem like a hypocrite. *Any* set of rules around how men and women should behave would do. The mere existence of any beliefs of the form—"men should be this way and women should be that way"—would be enough to render her worldview incoherent.

What neoracists really believe about the socially constructed character of race is something they reveal through their actions more than through their words. Even though they say that race is a social construct, their actions treat the concept of race the same way old-school racists do: as if race were a perfectly natural concept.

Humans have an inbuilt tribal instinct—a tendency to identify strongly with a group, to aim empathy inward toward its members and suspicion and hatred outward. That tendency appears to be baked into each of us at a biological level. That is our "hardware." The question is whether we use our "software"— cultural ideas, early childhood education, political discourse, art, media, entertainment, and so forth—to *amplify* our natural tendencies or *tamp down* on them. The neoracist mindset, wittingly or not, amplifies them.

I dream of a different society, one that recommits itself to the ideals that people like Martin Luther King Jr., Frederick Douglass, and Zora Neale Hurston defended and sometimes died for—a society that's stronger because of its commitment to fostering unity, not division; a society that doesn't promote racial stereotypes like DiAngelo, or racial discrimination like Kendi. It's a society that instead embraces our common humanity, one that recognizes that the way to move closer to achieving the goals we care about together is not by revitalizing race thinking but by extracting ourselves from its grip and ensuring our policies and institutions embody a commitment to colorblindness.

The War on Colorblindness

In 2014, while vacationing abroad with her family, Amélie Wen Zhao formulated the idea for her first novel, *Blood Heir*. Zhao loosely based it on the story of Anastasia, the Russian princess forced into exile by the execution of her family, but added several twists of her own, including magic, a racially diverse cast of characters, and a noble struggle against a brutal system of indentured servitude. With *Blood Heir*, she hoped not only to entertain but to draw attention to the real-word issue of human trafficking, especially as it existed in her home country of China.

Raised in Beijing before immigrating to America as an eighteen-year-old, Zhao had dreamed of writing young adult fiction since she was in kindergarten. But it was not until she participated in a Twitter pitch party—during which aspiring novelists can pitch their ideas to agents and publishers on social media—that she got her big break. A literary agent liked her pitch and signed her, eventually landing her a six-figure book deal with a major publisher. By January 2019, Zhao was teasing her hotly anticipated debut on social media and sending advance copies to book reviewers in preparation for its release that summer.

In a saner world, the release of *Blood Heir* might have been celebrated. But in our world, it was denounced. Why? In describing the system of indentured servitude portrayed in her novel, Zhao had unwittingly committed the sin of colorblindness. The public blurb for *Blood Heir* read as follows: "In a world where the princess is the monster, oppression is blind to skin color, and good and evil exist in shades of gray . . . comes a dark Anastasia retelling that explores love, loss, fear, and divisiveness and how ultimately it is our choices that define who we are."

The idea that nonracial oppression might exist, even in a fantasy world, offended some in the YA fiction community. In a scathing tweetstorm, the novelist L. L. McKinney charged Zhao with perpetuating anti-blackness and internalized racism. "Explain to me how you write a book pretty much about slavery and oppressions suffered by the Black community," McKinney demanded, "but 'oppression is blind to color.'" The social media mob piled on, accusing Zhao of everything from racism to the lesser, but still damning, charge of "tone deafness." Overwhelmed by the volume of criticism, Zhao released a statement explaining that her reference to colorblind oppression pertained to human trafficking in Asia, apologizing for harm caused, and canceling the publication of her novel until further notice.

Colorblindness is under attack. When I google "colorblindness, race," nine of the ten articles that appeared argue that colorblindness is wrongheaded, counterproductive, or racist. (The tenth is a Wikipedia page.) Public figures have learned the hard way that supporting colorblindness invites a torrent of punishment.

In 2020, actress Kristen Bell published a children's book called *The World Needs More Purple People*. The aim of the book was to help children focus on what people of different beliefs and backgrounds—the "reds" and the "blues"—have in common rather than what drives them apart. A "purple person," the result of mixing red and blue, was intended as a metaphor for someone who focuses on similarities over divisions. Ironically, her message proved divisive. Misunderstanding (perhaps intentionally) her metaphor as a statement about race, online critics accused her of promoting colorblindness. Bell scrambled to clarify that her book was not about race, and assured the social media mob that she opposed colorblindness.

In a 2019 radio interview, Senator Bernie Sanders suggested that voters should choose candidates "not by the color of their skin," but by "their abilities" and "what they stand for"—a classic expression of colorblindness. Years ago, such a statement would have been hailed as progressive. But instead of being praised, Sanders was mocked, most significantly by Stephen Colbert (the host of America's most popular late-night TV show), who sarcastically quipped, "Yes, like Dr. King, I have a dream—a dream where this diverse nation can come together and be led by an old white guy."

Had Colbert read what Dr. King had to say on the subject of political candidates and skin color, he might have held his tongue: "The basic thing in determining the best candidate," King wrote in his final book, "is not his color but his integrity."

It's an ironic feature of our national discourse that the resonance of Dr. King's message now depends entirely upon the identity of the messenger rather than the content of the message. In one study, behavioral scientist Michael Bernstein asked people to rate the following quote, squarely in the colorblind tradition, on a racism scale from 1 to 5 ("1" meaning not racist at all and "5" meaning extremely racist):

> Black supremacy is as dangerous as white supremacy, and God is not interested merely in the freedom of black men and brown men and yellow men. God is interested in the freedom of the whole human race.

The first group was told that the quote is by Dr. King (which is true) while the second group was told it was by President Trump (which is false). When participants believed it was a King quote, Republicans rated it a "1" and Democrats rated it a "1.3." In other words, almost nobody saw the quote as racist. But when participants believed it was a Trump quote, Republicans rated it a "1.4" and Democrats rated it a "3.4."

The general tone of public discourse about race displays alarming ignorance about colorblindness, which enemies of the dream have caricatured and villainized. Here's an example from Robin DiAngelo of one of the many grotesque misrepresentations of it:

> According to [colorblind] ideology, if we pretend not to notice race, then there can be no racism. The idea is based on a line from the famous "I Have a Dream" speech given by Dr. Martin Luther King . . . that one day he might be judged by the content of his character and not the color of his skin. . . . [This line] was seized upon by the white public because the words were seen to provide a simple and immediate

solution to racial tensions: pretend that we don't see race, and racism will end.

The philosophy of colorblindness doesn't claim that we can solve the problem of racism by pretending not to see it. Defenders of colorblindness see that racism continues to be a problem in America. In fact, they see the problem of racism in America more clearly than self-proclaimed "anti-racists" like DiAngelo. They see that you can't promote racial discrimination and racial stereotyping and claim in good faith to be anti-racist. They see that so-called anti-racists like DiAngelo are really just racists in disguise.

If anyone is blind to the problem of racism in America today, it's neoracists. Their blindness to their own racism and to the broader problem of racism in America is no accident. It's encoded in their very understanding of what racism is.

The commonsense definition of racism is what leaders of the civil rights movement consistently had in mind when they opposed the evil of racial discrimination. They saw clearly that racism can go in any direction—racists can be black or white, and that the targets of racism can be both white and black. In his last book, for instance, Dr. King defined racism as "a doctrine of the congenital inferiority and worthlessness of a people." He took for granted that people of all races could be racist toward one another. In one interview, he said that "black supremacy would be equally evil as white supremacy" and that "the cry 'black power,' whether they mean it or not, falls on the ear as racism in reverse."

Yet neoracists reject the commonsense understanding of racism at the heart of the civil rights movement. They redefine racism so that their own brand of racism doesn't count.

Neoracists claim that when white people are the targets of discrimination, stereotyping, and other forms of prejudice, hatred, or hostility, it doesn't count as racism. To qualify as racism, they say, the discrimination, stereotyping, prejudice, hatred, or hostility needs to be backed by power—which white people have and black people don't. As a result, neoracists insist that discriminating against white people on the basis of their skin color, promoting white stereotypes, and being prejudiced against white people and expressing hatred or hostility toward them on account of their race doesn't count as racism. Here's how DiAngelo puts it:

> People of color may also hold prejudices and discriminate against white people, but they lack the social and institutional power that transforms their prejudice and discrimination into racism; the impact of their prejudice on whites is temporary and contextual. . . . [O]nly whites can be racist . . . only whites have the collective social and institutional power and privilege over people of color.

If it were true that all white people have power and all black people don't, then there would be merit to the argument that discrimination coming from the powerful group had worse consequences than discrimination coming from the group without power.

But we don't live in a nation where white people have power and black people don't. At the time of writing, the top four most-populous cities in America all have black mayors. The vice president is black and the president was black not too long ago. There are black CEOs of Fortune 500 companies. Two of nine Supreme Court justices are black. Meanwhile, there are millions of white Americans who are not even powerful enough to command salaries above the poverty line.

Does the *average* white person have more power—on any given definition of power—due to higher average incomes and higher average wealth? Sure. But we don't experience our lives in terms of averages. We only ever experience our lives as unique individuals interacting with other unique individuals. If you're a white employee working for a black boss who exploits you in some way, what good is it to you that, *on average*, whites are more likely to be bosses? How could that fact about group averages possibly give you power in your particular situation?

The power dynamics between any two people is not predetermined by their race or by the average statistics of their group, as neoracists assume, but by their individual situations with respect to each other. This can and does vary widely with each unique situation. The neoracist effort to redefine racism therefore fails to capture the reality that we live in, and blinds them to the kind of racism they promote.

Race Supremacy Returns

Contrary to what neoracists claim, colorblindness is the only philosophy that enables us to recognize racism wherever it exists. Colorblindness embraces our common humanity—the conviction that what it takes for us to flourish has nothing essential to do with our skin color or our ancestry or any of the other traits that people use to define race. It is only by comparison to race-neutral treatment that anyone has ever been able to identify racism. Race neutrality is the benchmark against which racism has always been identified. In fact, it is probably the only benchmark against which racism could possibly be identified.

Neoracists want to have it both ways: They want to reject the philosophy of colorblindness, but they also want to condemn the injustice of anti-black racism. How do they pretend to do this if they reject the commitment to our common humanity that's the core of colorblind philosophy? The answer: They endorse a type of de facto race supremacy. Neoracists and white supremacists are both committed to different flavors of race supremacy. They both deny our common humanity. They both deny that all races are created equal. They both agree that some races are superior to others, and they both agree that not all people deserve to be treated equally in society.

White supremacists and neoracists might disagree about the details (who is superior and why), but they share a common racist anatomy. The biologist Robert Sapolsky provides a framework based on the research of Susan Fiske that's helpful for describing the difference between the racism of white supremacists and neoracists. Humans have a tendency for grouping people into "Us" versus "Them," and "Thems" evoke more complex feelings:

We tend to categorize Thems along two axes: "warmth" (is the individual or group a friend or foe, benevolent or malevolent?) and "competence" (how effectively can the individual or group carry out their intentions?).

Racists in the antebellum South often viewed black people as warm but incompetent—akin to children or the mentally handicapped. (Though some viewed them as cold and incompetent.) By contrast, anti-Semites in Europe often viewed Jews as cold but competent—that is, cunning, devious, and intelligent enough to run the world, yet also morally corrupt. The way neoracists view white people falls into this category. They accuse white people of being competent agents of evil—of having a disposition toward moral corruption even if they are otherwise competent, unlike black people and people of color generally, who are considered morally pure.

You might think race supremacy is too strong a term to describe what I'm talking about. Let me give two examples that I think merit it. In 2020, *The Cut*, an arm of *New York Magazine*, released a video to its ten million YouTube subscribers titled "So What Exactly Are White People Superior At?" In the video, an interviewer asks the titular question, and a rotating cast of respondents answer: "violence," "genocide," "being ignorant," "oppression," "letting their egos control their every move," "stealing people's lives," "being dicks," "gaslighting," "lack of empathy," "taking what's not theirs." The video was not framed as an interview with racists but as an interview of some cool people that had acceptable opinions—opinions that *The Cut* endorsed.

Another example comes from a Harvard University debate over affirmative action. Mired in a lawsuit alleging racial discrimination against Asian and white applicants to Harvard, the school hosted an event with the lead trial lawyer, Adam Mortara. As part of his argument, Mortara challenged the idea that any race of applicants could have better personality traits than any other—a key point of contention in the case:

> "No one—not Judge Burroughs, not Harvard—has ever explained how it is that African Americans and Hispanics just have much better objective personal qualities than white and Asian applicants," he said. "They've never done it."
>
> "I guess there's just something more personally appealing about African American and Hispanic applicants," Mortara quipped. In response, *at least a dozen students in the crowd voiced their agreement, shouting, "There is!"* (emphasis mine).

Michael Bernstein, the sociologist who performed the MLK-Trump experiment, found in another study that 55 percent of college students in his sample agreed with at least one of three quotes from Adolf Hitler's *Mein Kampf* once he swapped out the words "Jewish" and "white."

The animating feeling behind neoracism is that people of color are morally superior to white people—that people of color are better at being good people. That's at the core. The truth, which should be obvious, is that no race is morally superior to any other.

Whatever the differences in details, the similarities between white supremacy and neoracism show that both are incarnations of racism; both are committed to a type of race supremacy, and both promote the kind of racial tribalism that has marred and disfigured human societies throughout history.

The Neoracist Charade

It should be evident by this point that many self-proclaimed "anti-racists" are really just racists in disguise. Here are some of the key indicators we've discussed:

- They reject the explicit principles of civil rights leaders like Dr. Martin Luther King Jr.

- They endorse racial discrimination.

- They endorse racial stereotypes.

- They deny that the racial discrimination they promote is unjust and use racial stereotypes to justify it.

- They deny that the racism they promote exists and even redefine the term "racism" to support this contention.

- They deny our common humanity.

- They're committed to race supremacy.

In all of these respects, self-proclaimed "anti-racists" show themselves to be racists who don't differ fundamentally from white supremacists and racists of other kinds. There are two more indications that self-proclaimed "anti-racists" are really racists:

- They fail to support policies that would actually eliminate racism.

- They support policies that harm the racial minorities they claim they're trying to help.

An example that illustrates these two points is automated traffic enforcement.

Some cities have an automated system of traffic cameras that monitor motorists and issue tickets to those committing violations. The systems aim at increasing the safety of motorists, cyclists, and pedestrians, and they appear to be very effective at achieving that goal. The city of Chicago, for instance, saw a 64 percent spike in speed-related crashes citywide over a six-year period, yet areas monitored by cameras saw only an 18 percent increase. Similarly, during the same six-year period, the number of crashes resulting in serious injury or death increased 21 percent citywide but only 2 percent in areas monitored by cameras.

Saving lives isn't the only benefit of the cameras. They also eliminate the potential for human racial biases to play a role in stopping and ticketing violators. The cameras are installed proportionately in white and non-white neighborhoods, and because the system is automated, it removes human beings from the process of traffic enforcement. It eliminates, for instance, the potential for racial profiling or violence on the part of police officers conducting traffic stops.

Imagine how the past fifty years of race relations in the United States would've been different if cities and towns across the nation had used automated systems of traffic enforcement instead of police. How many bad interactions between police and citizens could have been avoided? If self-proclaimed "anti-racists" were sincere about eliminating racism from society, they would support automated systems like this that eliminate the potential for racial discrimination. But they don't.

When it turned out that black and Hispanic drivers were receiving more tickets than white drivers in Chicago, critics claimed that racial inequities were "baked into" the system, and called for it to be dismantled.

Their response follows a pattern that's typical of neoracists. They start by noting a racial disparity in the outcomes of a system or process—in this case, a difference in the number of traffic tickets issued to blacks and Hispanics in contrast to whites. Neoracists then claim that the disparity must be due to some type of racial discrimination. When they can't pinpoint a source for the discrimination, they claim that the racism is systemic—that it's not due to any individual or group of individuals but is instead "baked into" the system. But the traffic cameras are automated, which makes it impossible for neoracists to pinpoint a source for the alleged discrimination. They conclude that the discrimination is somehow built into the system independent of the actions or intentions of any individual people, and claim that the only solution is to dismantle the system as a whole. In its place, they propose an alternative that involves racial discrimination of a sort that they favor.

Later I'll discuss in detail the logical and factual errors that underwrite this line of reasoning. For the time being I'll simply note three things.

First, neoracists use the concept of systemic racism in these contexts to absolve themselves of any responsibility to prove an accusation of racism. We'll see later on that they employ a variety of other concepts to accomplish the same goal: the goal of preempting an honest, critical examination of whether their claims are true.

Second, when neoracists observe a racial disparity, they typically leap to the conclusion that it must be the result of some type of racism without considering any other possible explanations. In fact, some neoracists adopt this one-size-fits-all approach to explanation as a general principle. Consider Ibram X. Kendi's axiom: "When I see racial disparities, I see racism."

We needn't look far to see the absurdity of Kendi's logic. Consider a well-documented racial disparity: suicide rates. The white suicide rate in the United States is more than twice as high as the black rate or the Hispanic rate. According to Kendi's logic, this racial disparity in suicide rates must be evidence of systemic racism . . . against *white people*. If self-proclaimed "anti-racists" were sincere in their commitment to equality of outcome, wouldn't they be concerned with decreasing the white suicide rate?

Self-proclaimed "anti-racists" are insincere in their commitment to equal outcomes for all people in society. They never promote policies aimed at improving racial disparities, such as the suicide rate, in which whites are disadvantaged. Their lopsided approach to racial disparities reveals they are not really committed to equal outcomes per se. Their real commitment is instead to de facto race supremacy: a program in which all racial disparities must be eliminated except the ones that benefit people of color.

Which brings me to the third point: the policies that self-proclaimed "anti-racists" promote end up hurting the very people that they claim they're trying to help. Majority black and Hispanic neighborhoods in Chicago, for instance, witness a high number of serious and fatal car crashes due to speeding and red-light violations. The automated camera system has made it safer for residents of those neighborhoods. It has also decreased the likelihood of those residents having bad encounters with police officers. Dismantling the system would deprive residents of these benefits. Yet this is exactly what self-proclaimed "antiracists" propose.

Another example involves the effort to defund police departments. Advocates of the neoracist agenda have pushed to defund the police in many cities. They claim to be speaking on behalf of black Americans that black people want less police presence in their neighborhoods. Yet the numbers tell a different story.

A Gallup poll from 2020 showed that 81 percent of black Americans want the same (61 percent) or greater (20 percent) police presence in their own neighborhoods. Only 19 percent of blacks wanted less police presence—significantly fewer than the 28 percent of Asian Americans who said the same. It's easy to see why: 2020 saw the greatest single-year increase—30 percent—in the homicide rate in America in more than a century, a trend that disproportionately hit the black community. The factors contributing to the increase are not altogether clear, but it's likely some combination of general hostility toward police in the wake of George Floyd's murder, as well as efforts to defund and dismantle the police in some cities. (Because other nations did not see a similar spike in homicides, the pandemic is unlikely to be the cause.)

Shortly after Floyd's murder, the Minneapolis city council voted to "dismantle" the police. Many people (myself included) spoke out against this on the grounds that it didn't represent the general desires of people living in high-crime neighborhoods.

Later that year, the city council voted to divert $7.7 million away from the police department and toward other social programs—a move that I opposed for the same reason.

The result was predictable. Crime surged, harming the city's most vulnerable populations to a greater degree. The number of working police officers shrank from 851 to 638. Residents successfully sued the city for not maintaining the number of officers required in the city charter, citing the rise in violent crime as their main concern.

Ultimately, both decisions—to dismantle and to defund—were viewed as disastrous for the residents of Minneapolis and reversed by popular demand amid historic crime rates. In mid-2021, the city council approved $5 million in emergency funding to pay for police overtime. A few months later, the promise to dismantle the police was put to a referendum, where it lost by around 18,000 votes.

Neoracists support policies that are unpopular among black people as a whole. They support policies that hurt the people living in majority black communities. Yet they often act as spokespeople for the majority of blacks—and they're often treated that way by mainstream media—even though the policies they endorse contradict what black people actually want.

True Anti-Racism

True anti-racists don't promote racial discrimination and racial stereotypes. And true anti-racists don't try to justify racial prejudice, hatred, and hostility. They instead have the courage that inspired the civil rights movement: the courage, as we've seen, to oppose racial discrimination, stereotyping, prejudice, hatred, and hostility in all its forms. Neoracists like Kendi and DiAngelo try to capitalize on the anti-racist brand loyalty cultivated by the civil rights movement while changing the product formula and filling the can with garbage that directly contradicts the aims and principles of the abolitionists and civil rights activists of the past.

The following points should be uncontroversial to anyone who supports the true anti-racist legacy of the civil rights movement:

- Anti-racists remain committed to the explicit principles of civil rights leaders like Martin Luther King Jr.

- Anti-racists oppose racial discrimination.

- Anti-racists oppose racial stereotypes.

- Anti-racists oppose racial prejudice.

- Anti-racists oppose hatred and hostility directed at people because of their race.

- Anti-racists claim that all forms of racial discrimination are unjust and reject any attempt to use racial stereotypes to justify discrimination.

- Anti-racists embrace our common humanity.

- Anti-racists reject race supremacy.

- Anti-racists support policies that can actually eliminate racism.

- Anti-racists prioritize the well-being of concrete people and communities over the dictates of an abstract ideology.

These are the signs of true anti-racism in the mold of civil rights leaders, abolitionists, and opponents of Jim Crow. Anyone who tries to justify racial discrimination, stereotyping, prejudice, hatred, or hostility can't pretend to agree with either the letter or the spirit of the civil rights movement. If you keep these points clearly in mind, you won't be fooled by the sham anti-racism peddled by neoracists.

But how could self-proclaimed "anti-racists" and their supporters be as confused as I've made them out to be? And why do so many people continue to be fooled by the "anti-racist" label? The answer: theirs is the latest brand of bigotry to gain social approval in America, and that social approval acts as a buffer that insulates their views from scrutiny.

Every society contains people who champion bigotry and the sense of power and status it gives them. They enjoy feeling superior; they enjoy righteous anger; they enjoy receiving winks and back pats from other bigots in their tribe; and they enjoy ascending the tribal hierarchy by signaling their commitment to its bigoted ideals.

A healthy society stigmatizes this form of pleasure seeking. The threat of that stigma keeps people's desire for it in check. Stigmatizing bigotry and racial tribalism in all its forms is exactly what the philosophy of colorblindness does. Its across-the-board renouncement of bigotry is the only approach that's consistent with our common humanity. It's also the only approach that's practical in a multiracial society. No individual or group wants to become a target of bigotry. Hence, no individual or group should accept a social arrangement that exposes them to the threat of bigotry. Everyone in society thus has reason to favor stigmatizing bigotry in all its forms.

But societies often fail to stigmatize one kind of bigotry or another. When that happens, some bigots get their way, at least for a time, and the people they target suffer. Neoracism is the latest form of bigotry that American society has failed to stigmatize sufficiently. It's the latest form of socially approved bigotry.

Bigotry has the same shape wherever it appears, just a different orientation. There's always an in-group. And there's always an out-group that's the target of the in-group's hatred and hostility. For much of American history, the out-group targeted most was black people. And it was out of the heroic resistance to this pernicious bigotry that the principle of colorblindness was born.

2

The Real History
of Colorblindness

America was founded on an infamous contradiction. A fledgling nation that preached the value of freedom and equality simultaneously denied both to millions of African descent within its own borders. Indeed, American revolutionaries would often describe their relationship with Britain as akin to slavery, without noticing the irony underlying this charge.

Our foundational contradiction is well known by historians as well as by the general public. But there is another American contradiction, a more recent one, which is less often discussed: the fact that the colorblind principle, which formed the core of the fight against slavery and Jim Crow, was suddenly abandoned at the moment of its greatest victory. As the legal historian Richard Epstein memorably put it, the "ink was scarcely dry on the Civil Rights Act of 1964," which forbade the government as well as employers from taking race into account for any reason, when policies of racial discrimination began proliferating throughout the public and private sectors. In the historical blink of an eye, colorblindness transformed from an idea whose time had finally come into a symptom of moral backwardness—from a noble principle responsible for beating slavery and Jim Crow into a marker of evil.

In the half century since the victories of the civil rights movement, some of America's most celebrated scholars have been hard at work writing a false history of colorblindness. In their view, colorblindness was not the motivating principle behind the antiracist activism of the nineteenth and twentieth centuries but was instead an idea created by white racists, conservatives, and reactionaries. Kimberlé Crenshaw, for instance, has criticized the "color-blind view of civil rights" that she alleges "developed in the neoconservative 'think tanks' during the seventies." George Lipsitz, a black-studies professor at the University of California, writes that colorblindness is part of a "long-standing historical whiteness protection program" associated with "Indigenous dispossession, colonial conquest, slavery, segregation, and immigrant exclusion." According to these scholars, there is no contradiction to reconcile: colorblindness had nothing to do with abolition or the civil rights movement to begin with; colorblindness has instead always been a Trojan horse for white supremacy.

The purpose of this chapter is to set the record straight. Colorblindness was a key goal of the anti-slavery movement, and the main goal of the civil rights movement. It was not invented by conservatives or by racists. Rather, it was invented by the most radical anti-racist activists of the nineteenth and twentieth centuries, and then abandoned by the so-called anti-racists of our era.

THE ABOLITION OF SLAVERY

The earliest expressions of colorblindness came from the radical wing of the abolitionist movement, and in particular, from a man named Wendell Phillips. A prominent abolitionist and member of the American Anti-Slavery Society (ASA) during the 1840s and '50s, Phillips's prowess as a public speaker earned him the title "abolition's golden trumpet."

When slavery was finally abolished in 1865, Phillips clashed with the president of the ASA, William Lloyd Garrison. Garrison believed the ASA had completed its mission now that slavery was abolished, but Phillips, alongside Frederick Douglass, believed that the ASA should not be satisfied until black Americans had equal rights in all aspects of life. The ASA held a referendum on the question, and its members sided with Phillips, who replaced Garrison as the head of the ASA.

As the newly minted leader of the most important abolitionist organization in America, Phillips used his platform to propose a fourteenth constitutional amendment that would prohibit all state action based upon race—an amendment that would create, in his words, "a government color-blind." For nine months, he included the following post in every edition of the ASA's weekly newspaper:

PROPOSED AMENDMENT OF THE
UNITED STATES CONSTITUTION

NO STATE SHALL MAKE ANY DISTINCTION IN CIVIL
RIGHTS AND PRIVILEGES AMONG THE NATURALIZED
CITIZENS OF THE UNITED STATES RESIDING WITH
ITS LIMITS, OR AMONG PERSONS BORN ON ITS SOIL
OF PARENTS PERMANENTLY RESIDENT THERE,
ON ACCOUNT OF RACE, COLOR, OR DESCENT.

For Phillips, the true goal of the abolition movement was not simply the end of slavery but the destruction of the government's ability to make any distinctions among American citizens on account of race. Slavery may have been the most heinous example of race-based policy, but it was the destruction of race-based policies themselves that Phillips saw as the ultimate goal. As he put it during a speech in 1867:

> When once the nation is absolutely, irrevocably pledged to the principle that there shall be no recognition of race by the United States or by State law, then the work of the great anti-slavery movement which commenced in 1831, is accomplished.

In a speech given a few months later, Phillips reaffirmed that the ultimate goal of the anti-slavery movement was to achieve a colorblind state.

> God has chained this generation to the one great duty of eliminating from American politics the idea of *race*. When-

ever an American magistrate . . . is color-blind, unable to
distinguish white from black—when that day comes, the duty
of this generation is done and sealed, and this epoch is closed.

Wendell Phillips's version of the Fourteenth Amendment
would have created a colorblind government by prohibiting all
state action based upon race. Crucially, this would have made Jim
Crow laws and racial segregation presumptively unconstitutional.

But politics involves compromise. Elements of the Republican
party considered Phillips's proposal unacceptable. They felt that
returning to their white constituents and saying they had given
black Americans equal rights would be political suicide. So in the
final days of negotiation, the radicals who agreed with Phillips
were forced to compromise with the moderate elements of the
party. The result was the version of the Fourteenth Amendment
we have today—an amendment that guarantees only "equal protection." The stronger colorblind version of the amendment proposed by Phillips would have ruled out the very idea of "separate
but equal" institutions. The weaker version that was actually
ratified enabled the emergence of Jim Crow laws.

It is in the speeches given by Wendell Phillips that we find
the earliest advocacy for colorblindness—not by conservative
think tanks, white supremacists, or reactionaries but by a man
who led the most important abolitionist organization in American history—a man considered a radical in his time. It is fitting that
at his funeral in 1884, George Lewis Ruffin, America's first black
judge, said this: "In the eyes of many colored people, Mr. Phillips
was the one exceptional white American wholly color-blind and
free from race prejudice."

PLESSY V. FERGUSON

The constitutionality of segregation was challenged in the 1896 Supreme Court case *Plessy v. Ferguson*. The case concerned Louisiana's Separate Car Act of 1890, which required passenger trains to provide "equal, but separate" train cars for white and non-white passengers. A civil rights group, the Comité des Citoyens, decided to challenge the law. It convinced a mixed-race man, Homer Plessy, to violate the law by riding in the white-only train car. The Comité des Citoyens hired a private detective to arrest Plessy and ensure that he was charged with violating the Separate Car Act.

At trial, Plessy petitioned the judge, John Howard Ferguson, to throw out the case on the grounds that it violated the Fourteenth Amendment. Judge Ferguson nevertheless ruled that Louisiana had the right to regulate railroad companies within the state's own borders. The Louisiana Supreme Court later upheld Ferguson's decision, and the Comité appealed to the US Supreme Court. In May 1896, the Court upheld the constitutionality of the Louisiana law by a vote of 7 to 1.

The lone dissenting opinion was written by Justice John Marshall Harlan. It contains what is probably the most famous reference to colorblindness in American law:

Our Constitution is color-blind, and neither knows nor tolerates classes among citizens. In respect of civil rights, all citizens are equal before the law. The humblest is the peer of the most powerful.

But Harlan's arguments did not carry the day. Instead the court held that "separate but equal" provisions did not violate the Constitution because the Fourteenth Amendment did not rule out all distinctions based upon race—precisely the clause that Wendell Phillips had wanted to include some thirty years earlier.

Though Harlan's words did not persuade the rest of the court, they did inspire the generation of activists that would eventually bring down Jim Crow. His famous line—"Our Constitution is color-blind"—became the mantra of activists fighting segregation in the courts during the 1940s and '50s. An aide to Thurgood Marshall then, and a lawyer for the NAACP, recalled how much inspiration he drew from Harlan's words:

> [Thurgood] Marshall had a "Bible" to which he turned during his most depressed moments. . . . Marshall would read aloud passages from Harlan's amazing dissent. I do not believe we ever filed a major brief in the pre-Brown days in which a portion of that opinion was not quoted. Marshall's favorite quotation was, "Our Constitution is color-blind." It became our basic creed.

THE CIVIL RIGHTS MOVEMENT

One of the first major victories in the fight against segregation was achieved by a man named A. Philip Randolph. When we hear "March on Washington," we tend to think of the 1963 march (led by Randolph) where Dr. King delivered his famous "I Have a

Dream" speech. But the March on Washington movement was actually started by Randolph in the 1940s. In 1941, Randolph threatened a March on Washington if Roosevelt did not take action against racism. Roosevelt responded by integrating the war industries—a partial victory, but a victory nonetheless.

But not all of Randolph's demands had been met, and the March on Washington was his name for the movement aimed at achieving them. Randolph's March on Washington movement had a list of demands—first of which was "the abrogation of every law which makes a distinction in treatment between citizens based on religion, creed, color, or national origin"—nearly the exact wording of Wendell Phillips's proposed constitutional amendment some seventy-five years earlier. Randolph demanded, in other words, a colorblind government.

Colorblindness was a constant theme in the battle against Jim Crow in the 1940s. But the most significant legal challenge to Jim Crow didn't arrive until 1954: the Supreme Court decision in *Brown v. Board of Education*. State law prohibited Topeka, Kansas, resident, Oliver Brown, from sending his daughter to the local public school. It required her instead to ride a bus across town to a black school. The Browns and a dozen other families filed a class-action lawsuit against the Topeka Board of Education on the grounds that its segregation policy was unconstitutional.

The US District Court decided against the Browns. Their attorney, Thurgood Marshall, filed an appeal with the US Supreme Court. His argument opened like this:

The Fourteenth Amendment precludes a state from imposing distinctions or classifications based upon race and color alone.

The State of Kansas has no power thereunder to use race as
a factor in affording educational opportunities to its citizens.

This was "Point I" in his brief and was the main thrust of the
NAACP argumentation in *Brown* and in the other similar cases
in the lawsuit. You may notice that Marshall's argument employs
the same rationale used by Justice Harlan, A. Philip Randolph,
and Wendell Phillips. It even uses similar language to Phillips's
proposed Fourteenth Amendment.

But it was "Point II" in the NAACP brief that ultimately
swayed the Supreme Court. When it struck down school segregation in *Brown v. Board*, they did so not on the basis that the
Constitution is colorblind but instead based upon the claim that
segregated schools were "inherently unequal" because they lowered the self-esteem of black children, thereby depriving them of
equal protection under the law. And the Court made this argument
partly on the basis of a dubious social science experiment with dolls.

In 1947, Kenneth and Mamie Clark published their famous
doll study, titled "Racial Identification and Preference in Negro
Children." This study has gone down in history as one of the
most important social science studies of the twentieth century.
It worked like this: 134 black kids from southern, segregated
schools and 119 black kids from racially integrated northern
schools were presented with two white dolls and two black dolls.
They were given eight commands:

1. Give me the doll that you like to play with—(a) like best.

2. Give me the doll that is a nice doll.

3. Give me the doll that looks bad.

4. Give me the doll that is a nice color.

5. Give me the doll that looks like a white child.

6. Give me the doll that looks like a colored child.

7. Give me the doll that looks like a Negro child.

8. Give me the doll that looks like you.

According to the usual story, the results of this study showed that segregation lowered black kids' self-esteem, and Kenneth Clark's expert testimony in *Brown v. Board* helped persuade the court of this fact.

In the course of researching this book, however, I read the study in its entirety and was surprised to discover that its findings did *not* suggest that segregation harmed black kids' self-esteem. Quite the opposite. The kids who attended segregated southern schools had *higher* self-esteem than the northern kids who went to integrated schools. On every question relating to which doll is better, segregated kids fared better than integrated kids—by large amounts on commands 2 and 3, and by smaller amounts on commands 1 and 4. This is not only my analysis of the data. It is also the analysis reached by Kenneth and Mamie Clark in their own discussion section. (See Appendix C for the relevant table and text from the actual study, as well as a more detailed critique of its methodology.)

Many people who supported the *Brown* decision nevertheless objected to the rationale behind it. They saw it, as I do, as the right decision made for the wrong reason. Being in a monoracial environment, by itself, does not cause low self-esteem. To the extent that black Americans had low self-worth, it was not because of segregated schools per se but because of the wider cultural perception of blacks as lesser beings. Many blacks were proud of their all-black schools and saw them as incubators of high self-esteem—among them celebrated author Zora Neale Hurston, who wrote a scathing letter criticizing the rationale underlying the *Brown* verdict. To take one example, Dunbar High, a segregated public school in Washington, DC, outperformed white high schools in the same city on standardized tests.

So why did the Warren Court make its decision based on contingent empirical facts—such as whether segregated black schools provided subpar education? (Sometimes they didn't.) Or whether segregation lowers self-esteem? (It probably doesn't.) Why did they reach for a rationale based on dubious social science rather than strike down school segregation using the more straightforward argument that the state should be colorblind?

Though the historical record provides no direct answer, the legal scholar Andrew Kull hypothesizes that the Warren Court decided not to strike down school segregation on the basis of colorblindness because doing so would have simultaneously struck down every other Jim Crow law—a proposition they perceived, rightly or wrongly, as too extreme. Rather than risk the perception of judicial overreach and a dangerous backlash from the South, they made the pragmatic decision to strike down school segregation on narrow grounds, leaving other Jim Crow laws temporarily intact. It is worth noting the similarity between this pragmatism and the pragmatism that led Congress to forego the colorblind version of the Fourteenth Amendment. In both cases, the colorblind philosophy was not enshrined into law because decision-makers felt the need (rightly or wrongly) to compromise with the more racist elements of the country.

THE BETRAYAL OF COLORBLINDNESS

Though the *Brown* verdict was handed down in 1954, southern schools did not begin integrating in earnest until the passage of the Civil Rights Act of 1964. A landmark achievement, it outlawed discrimination on the basis of race, color, religion, sex, or national origin. While it fell short of prohibiting the state from drawing any distinctions based upon race, in every other respect it embodied the colorblindness that anti-racist activists had been fighting for throughout the past century.

During the Senate debate over the Civil Rights Act, southern Democrats expressed fears that the bill would lead not to a colorblind state but to racial discrimination in favor of blacks and against whites. But the language of the bill contained a clause that clearly stated the opposite: nothing in the law could be interpreted to require an employer to grant preferential treatment to anyone on the basis of underrepresentation of their race relative to any benchmark, such as the local or general population. In the Senate debate, supporters of the bill eagerly reminded its opponents of this fact. Senator Thomas Kuchel, a sponsor of the bill, called it "color-blind" with respect to preferential hiring. The bill's lead sponsor, Senator Hubert Humphrey, famously promised that if anyone could find a single sentence in the Civil Rights Act that required preferential hiring based on percentages or quotas, he would eat the entire bill page by page.

But by the early 1970s, the elite consensus had changed. The result was a strange and sudden pivot away from the colorblindness that had motivated the civil rights movement toward racial preferences. Institutions, from federal and state governments to labor unions to private corporations to colleges, began racially discriminating in precisely the ways that the sponsors of the Civil Rights Act had promised would not happen. The legal scholar Alexander M. Bickel described this odd pivot at the time:

> The lesson of the great decisions of the Supreme Court and the lesson of contemporary history have been the same for at least a generation: discrimination on the basis of race is illegal, immoral, unconstitutional, inherently wrong, and destructive of democratic society. Now this is to be unlearned and we are told that this is not a matter of fundamental principle but only a matter of whose ox is gored.

Why the sudden pivot away from colorblindness?

The answer has to do in part with the race riots that rocked cities like Detroit and Newark in the mid-1960s—especially during the summer of 1967. Many Americans were shocked to see black people rioting at the very moment when it seemed that the civil rights movement had achieved its greatest successes. They expected that the movement's success would have the effect of quelling civil unrest, but it did just the opposite. In the resulting confusion and dismay, people lost faith in the colorblind principle. If colorblindness could not prevent rioting, then what was it good for? (It is worth noting that whereas civil rights legislation transformed the *South*, the major rioting occurred in the *North*. So to view the riots as a negative comment on the achievements of the civil rights movement is, at best, oversimplified.)

In response to the rampant destruction, politicians wanted to be seen implementing policies to directly address the problems facing black ghettos—poverty, unemployment, police brutality, racism, and so forth—policies that put race on the front burner. Mayors appointed black police chiefs, changed hiring standards to bring in more black police officers and firefighters, and so forth. At the federal level, Richard Nixon rolled out a series of race-based "affirmative action" directives—initially called the "Philadelphia Plan"—that mandated government contractors to hit specific numerical goals with respect to the racial diversity of their workforce. In order to secure lucrative government contracts, for instance, Philadelphia iron trades had to be at least 22 percent non-white by 1973; plumbing trades had to be at least 20 percent non-white by the same year; electrical trades had to be 19 percent non-white, and so forth. Eventually, the Philadelphia Plan was extended to New York, Pittsburgh, Seattle, Los Angeles, St. Louis, San Francisco, Boston, Chicago, and Detroit.

None of these policies reflected the goals of the civil rights movement. Clarence Mitchell, the pro-colorblindness chief lobbyist of the NAACP, called Nixon's Philadelphia Plan a "calculated attempt . . . to break up the coalition between Negroes and labor unions." As Bayard Rustin, one of the lead architects of the

movement, reminded the public in 1974, "Quotas are the prog-
eny, not of the program of the civil rights movement, but rather
of the economic policies of the Nixon administration and of the
shortcomings of the administration's bureaucracy."

Leaders of the civil rights movement aimed at abolishing racial categories in the nation's entire legal regime. A. Philip Randolph's original March on Washington movement had atop its
list of demands the end of all race-based policies. The NAACP
lawyers who argued the *Brown* case wanted to prohibit the state
from making any distinctions based upon race. These historical
facts have been downplayed in an effort to avoid the depressing
conclusion that a significant portion of our society has betrayed
the ideals of abolition and the civil rights movement, even as we
pretend to celebrate them year after year.

REVERSE RACISM

The neoracist scholars who have claimed that colorblindness was
a cynical invention of white conservatives have made the same
claim about the concept of reverse racism. Neoracists believe that
reverse racism—racism against white people—is not possible even
in principle because racism requires institutional power, which
black people lack. Racism, they often say, equals prejudice plus
power.

In the effort to tarnish colorblindness as invalid, neoracist
scholars have branded the concept of reverse racism as a myth
invented by people who do not really care about racism. This is

simply not true. Many of our most celebrated anti-racist heroes believed reverse racism was real and was a cause for concern.

Dr. King, for instance, said that "black supremacy would be equally evil as white supremacy," and that "the cry 'black power,' whether they mean it or not, falls on the ear as racism in reverse." Roy Wilkins, the executive director of the NAACP, was even more critical. He called the Black Power movement, "a reverse Mississippi, a reverse Hitler, a reverse Ku Klux Klan."

Randolph made clear that his opposition to racism was not grounded in a *provincial* concern for racism against blacks in particular, but in a *universal* concern for racism as such. "Both black racism and white racism," he wrote, "are indefensible and dangerous to social peace and progress." He therefore called for "a moratorium on inflammatory racist propaganda against white people merely because they are white." As was the case with Randolph, Rustin opposed racial discrimination as such—not just racism against blacks. According to him, "The leaders of the civil rights movement—King, Randolph, Wilkins, and others—were explicit in opposing reverse discrimination."

Dismissing reverse racism as a concept invented by apathetic conservatives is not only historically inaccurate, it marks a rejection of the colorblind philosophy that motivated the entire American civil rights movement, and the philosophy that has motivated anti-racist movements around the world. That philosophy opposes racism in all its forms—both anti-black and anti-white. As late as 1995, Nelson Mandela—the hero of the fight against South African apartheid—criticized a university for practicing what he called "racism in reverse."

COMMON HUMANITY

A close cousin of colorblindness is the idea of common humanity: that there is only one race that really matters, the human race. What it takes for us to flourish has nothing essential to do with our skin color or ancestry or any of the other traits that people have used throughout history to divide themselves into racial groups. When we look at all the different ethnicities, races, and cultures of the world, we see that fundamentally people are more similar to one another than they are different—especially when it comes to the basic principles of human flourishing.

But neoracists of our era have made common humanity controversial once again. In 2015, the University of California released a document calling the phrase "There is only one race, the human race," a microaggression. Ibram X. Kendi says that the notion that there is "only one race, the human race" is "bound to fail" because it has "consistently failed in the past."

On the contrary, common humanity was the basis on which abolition and the fight against Jim Crow were fought—and won. Some of the most important anti-racist heroes of the nineteenth and twentieth centuries used the same phrases that Kendi and the University of the California believe we should rid from our vocabularies.

Frederick Douglass once told reporters, "I conceive that there is no division of races. God Almighty made but one race. . . . You may say that Frederick Douglass considers himself to be a member of the one race which exists."

Henry Highland Garnet, an escaped slave like Douglass, who holds the honor of being the first African American to speak at the nation's capital—which he did to honor the passage of the Thirteenth Amendment abolishing slavery—said this:

> In order to pursue my subject I must, for the sake of distinction, use some of the improper terms of our times. I shall, therefore, speak of *races*, when in fact there is but one race, as there was but one Adam.

Dr. King would often express the same idea, usually framed in religious language. "Racial segregation," he wrote, "is a blatant denial of the unity which we have in Christ; for in Christ there is neither Jew nor Gentile, bond nor free, Negro nor white."

Garnet, Douglass, King, and other leaders in the historic fight against racism embraced the idea that we are—all of us—united by our humanity, independent of our skin color, ancestry, or any other indicators of race.

A logical outgrowth of this belief in the unity of the human family is the belief that race is not an essential part of our identities—that race has nothing to do with who we are, deep down. Garnet, for instance, criticized those who "would draw a line of blood distinction, and would form factions upon the shallow basis of complexion."

Racist ideologies insist that race inevitably shapes our values and perspectives. But abolitionists and civil rights leaders throughout history have disagreed. They've argued that we can and should form our values and perspectives independent of race.

Douglass put it eloquently when asked if he fought for black people because he happened to be black:

> If I have advocated the cause of the colored people, it is not because I am a negro, but because I am a man. The same impulse which would move me to jump into the water to save a white child from drowning causes me to espouse the cause of the downtrodden and oppressed wherever I find them.

Bayard Rustin likewise clarified that his central role in the civil rights movement did not depend on his identity but upon his values:

> My activism did not spring from my being gay, or for that matter, from my being black. Rather it is rooted, fundamentally, in my Quaker upbringing and the values that were instilled in me by my grandparents who reared me. Those values are based on the concept of a single human family and the belief that all members of that family are equal. Adhering to those values has meant making a stand against injustice, to the best of my ability, whenever and wherever it occurs. The racial injustice that was present in this country during my youth was a challenge to my belief in the oneness of the human family. It demanded my involvement in the struggle to achieve interracial democracy, but it is very likely that I would have been involved had I been a white person with the same philosophy. Needless to say, I worked side-by-side with many white people who held these same values,

some of whom gave as much, if not more, to the struggle than myself.

Abolitionists like Douglass and Garnet, and civil rights leaders like King and Rustin who followed in their footsteps a century later, all emphasized common humanity and the corresponding irrelevance of race to the things we care about most in life. All of them saw race thinking as an obstacle to the dream of realizing a just society.

Every Martin Luther King Jr. Day, there are a predictable series of articles claiming that Dr. King was really a "radical"— especially toward the end of his life. The subtext of these articles is that if Dr. King were alive today he would support the policies and the rhetoric advanced by today's neoracist radicals—people like Kendi and DiAngelo. King's legacy, they argue, has been sanitized, co-opted, and weaponized by conservatives and moderates.

This argument relies on a bait and switch. The areas in which Dr. King could rightly be called a "radical" were twofold: economics and foreign policy. He favored policies like universal health care and guaranteed federal employment, and he strongly opposed the Vietnam War—positions that were considered radical in the 1960s.

Whatever you think of those positions, neither of them pertains to the topics on which he is alleged by modern commentators to have been a "radical"—namely, the importance of our common humanity and the goal of transcending race. On those topics, King never wavered. Nor did he waver on his preference for class-based policy over race-based policy. In his last book, he critiques the Black Power movement for focusing on race rather than class. He even suggests changing the slogan "Black Power" to "Power for Poor People."

In general, it is hard to imagine the radical neoracist thought leaders of today uttering even one of these Dr. King quotes, let alone all of them:

Let us be dissatisfied until that day when nobody will shout "White Power!"—when nobody will shout "Black Power!"—but everybody will talk about God's power and human power.

In an effort to achieve freedom in America, Asia, and Africa we must not try to leap from a position of disadvantage to one of advantage, thus subverting justice. We must seek democracy and not the substitution of one tyranny for another. Our aim must never be to defeat or humiliate the white man. We must not become victimized with a philosophy of black supremacy.

Black supremacy is as dangerous as white supremacy, and God is not interested merely in the freedom of black men and brown men and yellow men. God is interested in the freedom of the whole human race.

The problem is not a purely racial one, with Negroes set against whites. In the end, it is not a struggle between people at all, but between justice and injustice. Nonviolent resistance is not aimed against oppressors but against oppression. Under its banner consciences, not racial groups, are enlisted.

The important thing about man is "not his specificity but his fundamentum," not the texture of his hair or the color of his skin but the quality of his soul.

Properly speaking, races do not marry. Individuals marry.

As I stand here and look out upon the thousands of Negro faces, and the thousands of white faces, intermingled like the waters of a river, I see only one face—the face of the future.

If it strikes you as odd that today's neoracists sound nothing like Dr. King yet claim his mantle, it should. They do not carry his mantle. They enjoy the moral authority of being seen as the carriers of his legacy while simultaneously betraying the very ideals that he stood for.

3

Elite Neoracist Institutions

The neoracist in-group comprises many people in elite American institutions, such as colleges and universities, the mainstream media, and government. They've used the cultural power of these institutions to disseminate neoracist ideology.

The spread of neoracism within these institutions is clear from numerous examples. *The New York Times,* for instance, gave one of its journalists, Sarah Jeong, a pass for tweeting racist jokes about white people:

> "oh man it's kind of sick how much joy i get out of being cruel to old white men"

> "are white people genetically predisposed to burn faster in the sun, thus logically being only fit to live underground like groveling goblins"

Imagine if Jeong had tweeted about the joy she gets from being cruel to black people, or if she had suggested that black people be kept underground like groveling goblins. There can be little doubt that analogous tweets about black people—or probably any non-white group—would've gotten her fired. But her tweets expressed hatred and hostility toward white people, so she wasn't fired. *The New York Times* excused her racist tweets and continued supporting her.

Examples of neoracist double standards abound in the media, in government, in higher education, and increasingly in public education. In the chapters that follow, I discuss the ways in which neoracist ideology has infiltrated elite American institutions.

Some would argue that such double standards are justified because whites have power and blacks don't. Again, recall my argument from chapter one: we only ever experience our lives as unique individuals. The "average person" is a statistical abstraction. We don't ever experience having the average characteristics of our group; we experience having whatever level of power we, as *individuals*, in fact have. As you read about the following examples of neoracist policy, ask yourself: What "power" do the individuals discriminated against possess? What are they able to do that a similarly placed person of color could not do?

NEORACISM IN GOVERNMENT

How many government officials are actually true believers in neoracist ideology is anyone's guess. What we do know is that neoracist policies exist all throughout state, local, and federal governments. Because these initiatives are generally unpopular among voters, they are often downplayed and shrouded in euphemisms. Yet they keep appearing, and it is crucial that we examine their consequences with a close eye.

In March 2021, Congress passed a $1.9 trillion stimulus package: the American Rescue Plan. Section 1005 of the plan included $4 billion of aid for farmers with debt, but not just any farmers: only non-white farmers. White farmers with debt were to receive zero dollars of aid. Some of these white farmers faced foreclosure during the pandemic recession. They reasonably expected that if their government was going to distribute aid to farmers, it would do so according to who needed it most. They were understandably angry to learn that the government was distributing it instead according to skin color. Some of them sued the government, and a court ruled in their favor: distributing aid according to race, it said, was unconstitutional.

Yet the *New York Times*'s coverage of this episode didn't blame Congress or the Biden administration for passing a bill that was both racist and unconstitutional. It instead spun the story in a way that blamed the indebted white farmers—portraying them as angry conservatives who had ruined a noble government program and left black farmers in the lurch.

It is unreasonable to expect people of any race to sit idly by as laws get passed that openly discriminate against them on the basis of their race. That's why a colorblind legal regime is the best option for a multiracial society in the long run. If the Biden administration had passed a race-neutral bill aimed at helping all farmers with debt—and, if necessary, triaging them according to some objective measure of need, such as the size of their debt—it would have been more helpful and more just.

The Restaurant Revitalization Fund

Another part of the American Rescue Plan was the Restaurant Revitalization Fund. Approximately 73,000 restaurants closed in 2020 because of the COVID-19 pandemic. The fund earmarked $28.6 billion to support such restaurants; each business would receive up to $5 million in government aid. The Small Business Administration (SBA) would calculate the exact amount of aid based on the difference between the business's 2019 and 2020 receipts—essentially, the government would compensate the business for the amount of money it lost due to the pandemic.

All of this would have made sense, financially and ethically, except for the following provision: during the first three weeks of the program, only restaurants owned by veterans, women, and people of color could apply. This was known as the "priority group":

> For the first 21 days that the program is open, the SBA will prioritize funding applications from businesses owned and controlled by women, veterans, and socially and economically disadvantaged individuals.

"Socially disadvantaged" was synonymous with "non-white." And "economically disadvantaged" appeared to be a race-neutral category with eligibility requirements related to total assets and income, but in reality one had to be "socially disadvantaged" (and therefore non-white) in order to qualify as "economically disadvantaged."

Applications opened on May 3, 2021. Soon after, some white male restaurant owners filed a lawsuit, alleging unconstitutional racial discrimination—which it clearly was. By the time a judge ordered the SBA to stop its racial and gender triage, $18 billion of the $28.6 billion had already been given to the "priority group."

But it's not just white male restaurant owners who suffered as a result of this neoracist policy. Of the remaining $10 billion, some portion had already been promised to restaurant owners in the priority group and was then rescinded. Around 3,000 restaurant owners—women and people of color, mainly—were promised the money just *before* the court ordered the racist program stopped, and then un-promised the money, as if being punished for their former priority status. According to the SBA, the remaining $10 billion was then dispensed to the white male restaurant owners who had initially been put at the back of the line.

The funds dried up far quicker than the SBA anticipated. By May 24, the funds were gone and the applications closed. In the end, only 40 percent of eligible applicants received any money at all. It is a virtual certainty that there are former restaurant owners who didn't get aid simply because of their racial identity and went out of business as a result. Some of those people are white. Abstract notions about racism equaling "prejudice plus power" ring hollow in the face of this harsh reality.

The net result of the neoracist policy was a double dose of racial discrimination: initially thousands of white males were discriminated against, and then thousands of women and minorities were discriminated against. Can anyone argue that a race-neutral program based on financial need wouldn't have produced better results than the doubly racist mess that actually ensued?

Neoracist Medicine

Racialized public policy can mean much more than the difference between wealth and poverty. It can also mean the difference between life and death. During the pandemic, several government bodies recommended using race as a key variable in determining who received the vaccine first—even though this approach was guaranteed to lead to more overall deaths.

In November 2020, an official at the Centers for Disease Control and Prevention gave a presentation to the committee responsible for recommending the vaccine triage protocol. In her presentation, she acknowledged that giving the vaccine to the elderly first made more sense from the perspective of saving the most lives, as well as in terms of the feasibility of implementing the policy. Yet she ultimately recommended that we prioritize "essential workers," a category that encompasses everything from baristas to bank tellers, over the elderly because the elderly as a class are not racially diverse enough—too white, to put it bluntly. Though the result of this policy would likely have been thousands of needless deaths—including of many elderly black people—the committee unanimously accepted her recommendation. Thankfully, public outcry over the decision led to a last-minute reversal.

A year later, when successful COVID antivirals first became

available in limited supply, the New York Department of Health released official guidelines for who could receive them. Those guidelines included non-whites but required that white people have a separate medical condition or risk factor in order to receive them. To what extent these guidelines were actually followed is another question. But the mere fact that guidelines for distributing medicine were issued on racial lines is concerning.

All of these race-based policies were justified as attempts to close racial gaps in health outcomes. Black Americans died from COVID-19 at a higher rate than whites, a fact that commentators routinely attributed to systemic racism. Because racism was the cause, race-based policy should be the cure, the thinking went.

When black people are on the short end of a black-white health disparity, it automatically gets attributed to systemic racism. But when white people are on the short end of a black-white health disparity, few even notice the disparity and label it as such, much less attribute it to racism. White Americans are more likely than black Americans to die of chronic lower respiratory disease, Alzheimer's, Parkinson's, liver disease, and eight different types of cancer. The same thinking that automatically attributes the racial disparity in COVID-19 deaths to systemic racism against blacks could be applied equally to argue the existence of systemic racism against whites with respect to all of those diseases.

A fitting end for the saga of racialized COVID medicine: By late 2022, the racial profile of COVID-19 victims had switched. More whites were dying of it than blacks. Did systemic racism change its direction?

NEORACISM IN EDUCATION

Neoracist ideology has found a comfortable home in higher education. Yale University's Child Study Center, for instance, invited the psychiatrist Aruna Khilanani to deliver a talk in April 2021 titled "The Psychopathic Problem of the White Mind." Khilanani endorsed numerous white stereotypes in her talk. She claimed, for instance, that "White people are out of their minds and they have been for a long time" and compared them to "a demented violent predator who thinks they are a saint or a superhero." What was most striking about Khilanani's talk, however, was that she described her fantasies about murdering white people:

> I had fantasies of unloading a revolver into the head of any white person that got in my way, burying their body and wiping my bloody hands as I walked away relatively guiltless with a bounce in my step, like I did the world a fucking favor.

University administrators debated whether to post the video. They were committed, they said, to freedom of expression, but they also had grave concerns about the talk's tone and content—in particular, the speaker's "extreme hostility, imagery of violence, and profanity." Conspicuously absent from their list of concerns was the speaker's racism—that she had targeted a particular racial group for her extreme hostility and violence. That absence suggests that if Khilanani hadn't talked about shooting and hadn't used the word "fucking," the Yale administration might not have raised an eyebrow.

To appreciate how shocking Yale's response is, suppose Khilanani had described fantasies about shooting black people in the head, burying them, and walking away with a bounce in her step. Is there any doubt that the Yale administration would have condemned her racism in addition to her hostility, violence, and profanity? But Khilanani described fantasies about murdering white people not black people, and that expression of anti-white racism, it seems, didn't merit condemnation.

Statements like Jeong's and Khilanani's are exactly the kinds of things that racists have always said to each other in private. What's surprising isn't that racists would say these things to each other; what's surprising is that they can now say these things in public, with the implicit endorsement of institutions like Yale University and *The New York Times*—institutions that are willing to provide platforms that extend the reach of neoracist ideology throughout American society.

Racial Segregation on Campus

Another example of neoracism in higher education is the reintroduction of racial segregation on college campuses. The National Association of Scholars published a report in 2019 titled "Separate but Equal, Again: Neo-Segregation in American Higher Education." It surveyed 173 four-year colleges and universities across the country and found that 43 percent offered racially segregated dorms, 46 percent had racially segregated student orientation programs, and 72 percent had racially segregated graduation ceremonies. (To be clear, not all dorms, orientation programs, and graduation ceremonies on these campuses are racially segregated. Most are not. But the fact that they offer segregated spaces as an option is troubling enough.)

Higher education's embrace of racial segregation is ironic for two reasons. First, it marks a clear rejection of the principles of the civil rights movement—a movement that was committed to fighting and ending racial segregation in our country. Second, the policies that are now in place at many elite colleges and universities line up with the segregationist agenda of white nationalists.

Jared Taylor, for instance, is a white nationalist who celebrates white race consciousness and race thinking at large. He thinks that the experiment of having an integrated multiracial society has failed. When races live together, he thinks, they will inevitably come into conflict—too much conflict for racial intermingling to be worth the trouble:

> The persistence of black racial consciousness in the face of sincere white efforts to practice race-blindness and even preferential treatment for minorities is the single greatest failure of racial liberalism, and the most certain sign that those who have promoted it do not understand human nature or the world in which we live. It is only a matter of time: Black racial consciousness—together with Hispanic and, to a lesser extent Asian consciousness—is reawakening white racial consciousness.

Taylor's embrace of racial tribalism should seem regressive to anyone who's supported the goals of the civil rights movement. Yet many elite colleges and universities embrace reasoning similar to Taylor's: the experiment of having an integrated multiracial student body has failed, they think. We need to protect students from racial conflict, which is the inevitable result of interracial contact. The only solution is to have racially segregated options for students of color—"safe spaces" where white people can't hurt them.

During the 1960s, Kenneth Clark, the father of the *Brown v. Board* doll experiment, served on the board of trustees of Antioch College. When the college instituted segregated facilities that excluded white students, he wrote a scathing criticism and resigned, saying that he opposed it "for the same reasons that we fought together in the school segregation cases which led to the *Brown* decision."

If diversity is to have any legitimate value for higher education, that value must derive from exposing students to people, ideas, cultures, and viewpoints different from their own. Introducing segregation into institutions of higher education cuts against this mission. It artificially restricts their experience of the world in a way that is contrary to the goals of higher education.

Segregated dorms, study programs, clubs, and graduation ceremonies go directly against the educational goal of broadening students' horizons. It undermines the only legitimate rationale for promoting diversity in the context of higher education. Not to mention that it also lines up with the logic of white separatism. The reintroduction of segregation is just one indication, among many, of how entrenched neoracist ideology has become in higher education.

Racial Discrimination in Hiring

For the past half century, university and corporate hiring has exhibited a kind of doublethink. On the one hand, there has been a mandate to immediately increase the number of non-white employees or else the institution is deemed racist. But on the other hand, every individual hire must be seen as merit-based, or else the hired employee will lack the respect of his or her peers, and the candidates who were passed over will feel the sting of discrimination.

Inevitably, these two demands sometimes conflict. When they do, the solution has generally been to insist, dishonestly, that both demands have somehow been met, leaving observers to puzzle, like a magician's audience, at how this could possibly be.

But sometimes this strategy is not possible. Sometimes, the violation of merit is done openly for all to see. Take, for instance, Texas A&M, America's largest public university. In July 2021, Texas A&M set aside $2 million available only for new non-white hires. In addition to being a likely violation of civil rights law, it is an open rejection of meritocratic hiring in favor of race-based hiring. Every hire admitted under such a program will work under an unspoken cloud of suspicion, a quiet understanding that they may not be the best available person for the job. The candidates rejected because of their race may never forget or forgive the perceived injustice against them. And the students may even quietly suspect that they've been subjected to a subpar professor. If this is the status quo we have chosen as a nation, then we should acknowledge that it comes at a great cost.

Neoracism in K–12 Public Education

In March 2022, the Minneapolis Public School District signed a contract with the Minneapolis teachers' union that introduced what they called "protections for educators of color." The new contract replaces seniority with race as a criterion for staffing decisions. It requires Minneapolis public schools to lay off or reassign white teachers before taking the same action with nonwhite teachers.

Previously, budgetary layoffs and reassignments were based on seniority: the last person hired was the first to be laid off. Yet according to the new contract, it is not the last person hired but the last *white* person hired who is the first to be laid off. "The purpose of [the new policy]," the contract says, "is to remedy the continuing effects of past discrimination by the District."

Some heralded the new contract as a victory for people of color. The Associated Press wrote, "When Minneapolis teachers settled a 14-day strike in March, they celebrated a groundbreaking provision in their new contract that was meant to shield teachers of color from seniority-based layoffs and help ensure that students from racial minorities have teachers who look like them." The new contract is indeed a victory—for neoracists. It's another example of the success they've had infiltrating the educational system in America.

Another example of neoracist influence in K–12 public education comes from New York City. In 2018, the NYC Department of

Education earmarked $23 million for mandatory "anti-bias" training for the city's teachers over the course of four years. Leading this charge was chancellor of schools Richard Carranza, whose philosophy has less to do with eliminating actual racism than with eliminating so-called white supremacy culture in schools. In a presentation to top administrators, Carranza called for an end to all aspects of white supremacy, including "a sense of urgency," "worship of the written word," "perfectionism," "individualism," and "objectivity." Instead of these false values, he argued that teachers should prioritize non-white values like "the ability to relate to others."

The idea that perfectionism, objectivity, and good grammar belong to white people and shouldn't be taught to blacks and Hispanics is exactly the kind of idea that leaders of the civil rights movement fought against. There is nothing anti-racist about this idea. It is, at its core, racist.

On a practical level, moreover, poor children with less-educated parents and chaotic home lives are the ones who *most* need a school environment in which expectations are high and discipline is consistent. More so than kids with highly educated parents and privileged upbringings, they may never know the extent of their own academic talents until they are asked to rise up and meet a high bar.

NEORACISM IN MEDIA

A few years ago, a man was killed by police when an officer restrained him by kneeling on him with most of his body weight for over ten minutes. There were signs that the man was in distress, but the officer persisted, and the man lost consciousness and eventually died. The brutal affair was captured on video.

You might be thinking of George Floyd, but that's not the man I'm talking about. I'm talking about Tony Timpa. He was killed in Dallas on August 10, 2016. Unlike George Floyd's death, Tony Timpa's was barely newsworthy as far as the national media was concerned. Unlike George Floyd, Tony Timpa was white.

Despite the enormous media attention given to police violence since roughly 2013, many Americans are still unaware that every year, several dozen unarmed white Americans are shot by the cops—a higher total number than unarmed blacks killed by the cops.

At the height of the George Floyd and Breonna Taylor protests in 2020, I wrote an essay for *City Journal* titled "Stories and Data." I picked a random recent year—2015—and listed just some of the unarmed white Americans killed by cops that year:

1. Timothy Smith was killed by a police officer who mistakenly thought he was reaching into his waistband to grab a gun; the shooting was ruled justified.

2. William Lemmon was killed after he allegedly failed to show his hands upon request; the shooting was ruled justified.

3. Ryan Bolinger was shot dead by a cop who said he was moving strangely and walking toward her; the shooting was ruled justified.

4. Derek Cruice was shot in the face after he opened the door for police officers serving a warrant for a drug arrest; the cops recovered marijuana from the property, and the shooting was ruled justified.

5. Daniel Elrod robbed a dollar store, and, when confronted by police, allegedly failed to raise his hands upon request (though his widow, who witnessed the event, insists otherwise); he was shot dead. No criminal charges were filed.

6. Ralph Willis was shot dead when officers mistakenly thought that he was reaching for a gun.

7. David Kassick was shot twice in the back by a police officer while lying face down on the ground.

8. Six-year-old Jeremy Mardis was killed by a police officer while sitting in the passenger seat of a car; the officer's intended target was Jeremy's father, who was sitting in the driver's seat with his hands raised out the window.

9. Autumn Steele was shot dead when a police officer, startled by her German shepherd, immediately fired his weapon at the animal, catching her in the crossfire. Shortly after he killed her, bodycam footage revealed the officer's despair: "I'm f—— going to prison," he says. The officer was not disciplined.

I can virtually guarantee that you've never heard a single name on the above list. But I'm sure you've heard of names like

Tamir Rice, Alton Sterling, Philando Castile, Sandra Bland, Michael Brown, and Eric Garner. There is one reason for that, and it is the skin color of the victims.

Someone might object, "But, Coleman, you're overlooking an important historical fact: for most of American history, it was white suffering that provoked more outrage than black suffering. Now the tables have turned. It's hard for many people to feel the same level of outrage when they hear about cops killing a white person. And that is as it should be given the history of black suffering in our country."

If this new anti-white bias is justified—if we should accept a concept of justice based on racial-historical bloodguilt, and if we should care about some lives more than others based on their skin color, as racists of all sorts have long claimed—then everything that leaders of the civil rights movement thought about basic morality, and everything that the world's philosophical and religious traditions have been saying about revenge and forgiveness since antiquity, should be thrown out the window.

Someone else might object, "Coleman, police kill plenty of unarmed white people, but it's the ratios of the killings that count. Police kill more unarmed black people relative to the number of black people in the general population. Between 2015 and 2023, 459 unarmed Americans were killed by the cops; 148 were black. Therefore, black people, who comprise 14 percent of the population, account for 32 percent of the unarmed Americans killed by police. That disproportionality suggests racial bias."

This objection commits a basic error in statistical reasoning. To demonstrate the existence of a racial bias, it's not enough to observe a disparity between the percentage of unarmed black

Americans killed by police and the percentage of black people in the general population. Applying that logic, you could prove that police shootings were extremely sexist because men account for only 50 percent of the population but 92 percent of the unarmed Americans killed by police.

To reason correctly about the data, you need to do what good social scientists do: control for confounding variables to isolate the effect that one variable has upon another—in this case, the effect of a suspect's race on a cop's decision to pull the trigger. At least three careful studies have done this—one by Harvard economist Roland Fryer, one by a group of public-health researchers, one by economist Sendhil Mullainathan. None of them has found a racial bias in deadly shootings.

But even though these studies haven't found a racial bias in police shootings, that doesn't mean there are no racist cops and no problems of racial bias in the police. Fryer's study, for example, also found an anti-black bias in the use of *non-lethal* force on black suspects. The police, in other words, are more likely to rough you up if you're black, but no more likely to pull the trigger.

One thing is clear about police brutality: we want to stop it from happening—to anyone. Yet for the past decade the stories that the media has given national coverage involve black victims even though there have been more cases each year involving white victims. It is tempting to justify the media bias by saying that black victims deserve some extra consideration. But the ultimate irony is this: Think about what might have happened if the Tony Timpa case had gotten national media attention. Police departments might have begun prohibiting the practice of kneeling on people's necks, just as they began prohibiting choke holds after the case of Eric Garner. Had Tony Timpa's death received more attention and more outrage, there is a decent chance that George Floyd would still be alive today.

The 1619 Project

The 1619 Project is a *New York Times* initiative spearheaded by the journalist Nikole Hannah-Jones. It comprises a series of articles that aim to retell the story of America's founding by placing slavery at the story's center. The project was launched in 2019 to commemorate the four hundredth anniversary of the year the first African slaves arrived in colonial Virginia.

The project includes materials for use in K–12 school curricula, and some of the country's largest school districts—including Buffalo, Chicago, New York, Wilmington, NC, and Washington, DC—have adopted materials from it. And, in 2020, Nikole Hannah-Jones won a Pulitzer Prize for her introductory essay. The only problem: what the essay said was incorrect.

According to Hannah-Jones's essay, "one of the primary reasons the colonists decided to declare their independence from Britain was because they wanted to protect the institution of slavery." Colonists, she alleged, were afraid that the British would soon force them to give up their slaves. Leslie M. Harris, a historian who was enlisted by the *Times* to fact-check the project, said that she had "vigorously argued against" the claim that the revolution was fought to preserve slavery, since slavery in the colonies was not under threat by Great Britain. Harris adds that the opposite is true: the Revolutionary War disrupted slavery in the colonies. But *The New York Times* ignored her:

> Despite my advice, the *Times* published the incorrect statement about the American Revolution anyway, in Hannah-Jones' introductory essay. In addition, the paper's characterizations of slavery in early America reflected laws and practices more common in the antebellum era than in Colonial times, and did not accurately illustrate the varied experiences of the first generation of enslaved people that arrived in Virginia in 1619.

The *Times* moved forward with the publication of Hannah-Jones's essay even though historians—including one of their own chosen consultants—had demonstrated its inaccuracy.

Nearly as bad was Hannah-Jones's claim about who it was that fought back against slavery and Jim Crow: "For the most part," she claimed, "black Americans fought back alone." The "for the most part" makes for the illusion of nuance and creates an escape hatch from critique. But the claim is still wildly misleading. On her account, it's as if the abolitionist Quakers, the American Anti-Slavery Society, various state and local anti-slavery societies, Elijah Lovejoy, William Lloyd Garrison, John Brown, Wendell Phillips, Harriet Beecher Stowe, and the Grimké sisters never existed. And that's not to mention the white Americans who participated in the civil rights movement. For neoracists like Hannah-Jones, white participation in the fight against slavery and Jim Crow must be downplayed because whiteness must always and everywhere equate to evil.

Wokewashing in Hollywood Films

People have used the term "whitewashing" to refer to efforts to downplay the contributions of people of color in history, or to downplay the sins of white Americans. Historically, this has been a real problem in American culture. But today the trend is the opposite. I call it "wokewashing." Wokewashing occurs in one of two ways: either it exaggerates wrongdoings of white people or it downplays the wrongdoings of people of color. These days, big-budget Hollywood films routinely wokewash history. Take two examples.

The recent film *The Woman King* depicts an all-female military unit that fought on behalf of the Kingdom of Dahomey—a West African tribe that controlled a large part of modern-day Benin between the seventeenth and twentieth centuries. The film stars Viola Davis, who plays the leader of the military unit—a character who heroically opposes the slave trade. But in reality the Dahomey military leaders were unanimous in their support of slavery. Capturing other Africans and selling them to Europeans was one of the main sources of their wealth. Not only did they wage war precisely to obtain and sell slaves, they also kept slaves for themselves to work on their plantations. As one historian put it, "More than any other African state, Dahomey was dedicated to warfare and slavery."

The 2016 film *Hidden Figures* provides another example. It tells the story of an all-black group of female mathematicians who worked at NASA during the early 1960s. The film depicts the mathematicians Mary Jackson, Dorothy Vaughan, and Katherine

Johnson being forced to use segregated bathrooms and dining facilities as late as 1961. But the real-life Katherine Johnson stated in an interview that she "didn't feel any segregation" at NASA. Did the filmmakers fail to consult Johnson about her experiences? Or did they know about Johnson's experiences and choose to wokewash them anyway? According to the strange dictates of neoracism, whiteness is inherently evil and blackness is inherently good. That's why the Dahomey could not be portrayed as the slave-raiding, slave-trading tribe that they in fact were, and it's why Katherine Johnson had to experience more segregation than she in fact did.

Neoracism was once a fringe ideology believed by a few radical academics and activists—a belief system without any real currency in wider society. I hope the previous chapter has convinced you that this is no longer the case. Neoracism now infects most of our major institutions: government, education, media, and more. The question remains: How did neoracism go from a fringe belief system into the mainstream? This is the question that we turn to next.

4

Why Neoracism Is Spreading

Neoracist ideology has spread rapidly through American society over the past decade.

Zach Goldberg, a researcher at the Manhattan Institute, has compiled what he calls the Woke Term-Usage Index—a measure of the frequency with which various media sources use terms like "systemic racism" and "whiteness." His data show that the use of such terms has skyrocketed in the past decade.

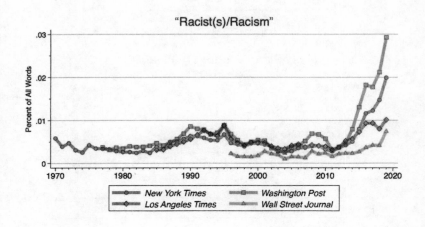

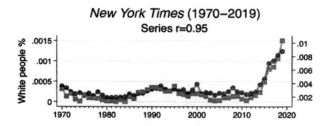

New York Times (1970–2019)
Series r=0.95

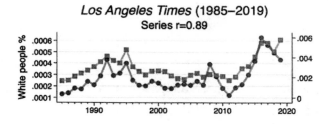

Los Angeles Times (1985–2019)
Series r=0.89

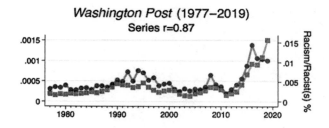

Washington Post (1977–2019)
Series r=0.87

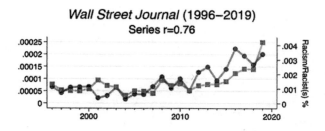

Wall Street Journal (1996–2019)
Series r=0.76

"White people"   "Racism/Racist(s)"

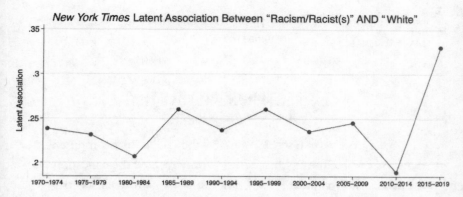

New York Times Latent Association Between "Racism/Racist(s)" AND "White"

SOURCE: Zach Goldberg, "How the Media Led the Great Racial Awakening," *Tablet Magazine.*

What has caused neoracist ideas to spread over the past decade?

Some trends in recent American history have set the stage for the rise of neoracism. The first is the end of the Cold War and the declining importance of the War on Terror. The end of these conflicts has created a situation in which the United States no longer has a scary foreign enemy to fight. The absence of a common enemy has magnified the importance of domestic conflicts.

Second, the decline of Christianity in American culture—which has been beneficial in many ways—has created an ideological vacuum into which neoracism has been able to enter. The common humanity and anti-racism of the civil rights movement had strong ties to Christianity. And Christianity promoted the value of interracial harmony: unity in Christ. But the appeal of Christianity has since waned—especially among liberal white Americans and young black Americans, and the resulting vacuum has given neoracism—a far more racially divisive ideology—a place to settle.

THE SMARTPHONE REVOLUTION

The conditions I've described so far—the lack of a common enemy and the decline of Christianity—only created the conditions for neoracism to spread. They don't fully explain what has triggered its growth over the past decade. There's more to the story.

The chart below is perhaps the single most shocking graph relating to American race relations that I am aware of. Gallup has been asking both white and black Americans their opinion on the status of race relations every year since at least 2001 to the present. Here is the result:

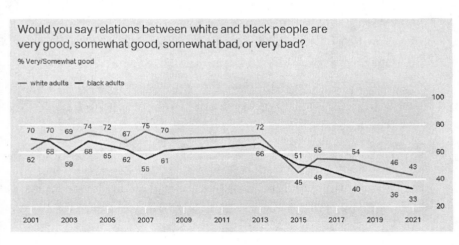

Would you say relations between white and black people are very good, somewhat good, somewhat bad, or very bad?

% Very/Somewhat good

— white adults — black adults

SOURCE: Gallup, "Race Relations," news.gallup.com/poll/1687/race-relations.aspx.

The Bush years and early Obama years represented a fairly healthy equilibrium for America on the issue of race. The majority of Americans—both black and white—believed that race relations were good. Then, after 2013, something changed. Around that time American attitudes toward race relations took a nosedive. By 2021 about half as many Americans felt that we were in a good place as felt that way in 2013.

It's not an exaggeration to say that whatever happened after 2013 represents the biggest setback in American race relations in at least a generation.

So what happened? Why did people's attitudes toward race relations take a nosedive in 2013? We can rule out a few explanations. It probably was not the election of President Obama, since he presided over five years of good race relations. And it probably wasn't President Trump either, as the downward trend began three years before he was elected, and hasn't reversed itself since his departure from office. As much as we like to blame presidents for everything, the reality is that sweeping social trends have causes that run deeper than a single individual.

We can also rule out the idea that actual racism suddenly increased in 2013. If there had been an uptick in the popularity of white supremacy or an uptick in the number of unarmed black people shot by police, then we'd have reason to suspect that there was an increase in racism. But neither of those is the case. Support for white supremacy has been steadily declining for decades, and so has the annual number of police shootings.

The more plausible explanation is that 2013 is about the time that a critical mass of Americans had two pieces of tech:

camera-enabled smartphones and social media. The widespread use of social media and smartphones increased the speed at which content could spread throughout the world. But not all content was able to take advantage of this development equally. Neoracist ideas were able to take advantage of this development in a way that other ideas could not.

Here's an analogy: Imagine that the speed limit on a highway was suddenly raised from 75 mph to 200 mph. Not all cars would be able to take advantage of this change. If you drive a Chevy Spark (with a top speed of 89 mph), the new speed limit change wouldn't benefit you much. But if you drive a McLaren Speedtail (with a top speed of 250 mph), you'd suddenly be able to travel much faster.

What happened around 2013 is that the speed limit on the information highway was suddenly raised—not by a factor of two or three, but by several orders of magnitude. And it turns out that certain content has a much higher "top speed" than other content. Anything that appeals to our tribal identities, us versus them narratives, or historical grievances travels fast. These pieces of content are the McLarens of the internet. Anything that emphasizes common humanity, rational analysis, or fact-checking, on the other hand, travels far more slowly. These are the Chevy Sparks.

When Michael Brown was killed by Darren Wilson in Ferguson in 2014, the narrative that a racist cop had killed an unarmed black teenager who had his hands up spread quickly. As far as narratives go, this one tapped into every psychological trigger that would lead people to share it widely: black v. white, histori-

cal grievances, violence, and so on. The fact-check of this event—
that Michael Brown did not have his hands up, had physically
overpowered the officer, punched him, and tried to steal his
gun—traveled slowly because it appealed more to reason than to
outrage. Indeed it traveled so slowly that it still has not reached
the countless individuals who, years later, still believe the mythical
version of events. To this day, "Hands Up, Don't Shoot" remains
one of the most popular slogans at Black Lives Matter protests.

Back when all information spread more slowly, the fact-
checked version of events could arrive in time to preempt false
representations (the Chevy and the McLaren arrived at the same
time). But those days are over. In an age with so many content
creators and content distributors, myths and half-truths can easily outrun the facts. Neoracist ideology—because it casts every
event as an instance of us versus them, good versus evil, black
versus white—has been able to take advantage of the increased
speed and decreased quality of the information people circulate.

The majority of black Americans pre-2013 believed that race
relations were good. Consider the chart on the next page, which
tracks the percentage of black Americans who believe that racial
discrimination was the main issue causing disparities in housing,
jobs, and income:

Blacks' Views of Discrimination

On the average, blacks have worse jobs, income, and housing than whites. Do you think this is mostly due to discrimination against blacks, or is it mostly due to something else?

■ % Mostly discrimination   ■ % Mostly something else

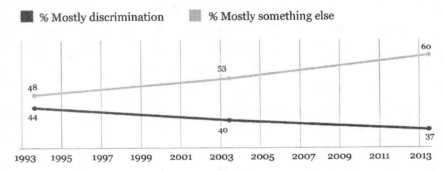

SOURCE: Gallup, "Fewer Blacks in U.S. See Bias in Jobs, Income, and Housing," news.gallup.com/poll/163580/fewer-blacks-bias-jobs-income-housing.aspx.

As late as 2013, a clear majority of black Americans did *not* think that discrimination was the main driver of racial disparities. That is back when people were judging societal issues mainly by reference to their own lived experience—in addition to a slow-moving information diet that consisted of reading newspapers and watching the news on TV.

Prior to 2013, most blacks and whites in America thought race relations were good. The trend line showed that fewer and fewer blacks every year saw racial discrimination as a big issue. Then everything changed. We saw a tenfold increase in mentions of race and racism—despite every indication that viewpoints about actual racism against blacks was trending downward.

Why, then, did people's perception of race relations take a nosedive after 2013? The answer is that smartphones and social media changed the speed limit of information—which in turn gave a massive competitive advantage to ideas, information, narratives, and arguments that tap into division, tribalism, and grievances. Neoracism was among the ideologies able to take advantage of this seismic change. Ultimately, this change resulted in an information diet that is *less* tethered to reality, not more.

Correlational data show that black people who use social media are more likely to report being victims of racial discrimination than black people who don't. Correlation does not imply causation. But the data, at least, are consistent with the view that social media has caused a major shift in how people view themselves and the world—a shift away from reality and toward paranoia, pessimism, and catastrophizing.

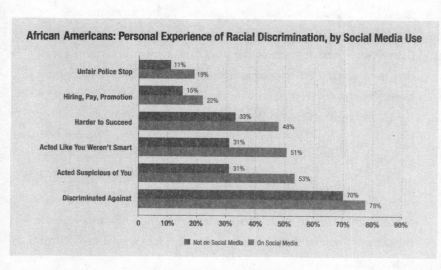

African Americans: Personal Experience of Racial Discrimination, by Social Media Use

SOURCE: Eric Kaufmann, "The Social Construction of Racism in the United States," Manhattan Institute, April 2021. Calculated by Eric Kaufmann from *2016 Racial Attitudes in America Survey* data set, Pew Research Center (conducted February–May 2016); file released July 27, 2017.

The news doesn't report on the millions of black people who never encounter racism in their daily lives. Their experiences aren't newsworthy. The upshot: the media is heavily biased toward reporting emotionally charged stories of racism—stories that create a misperception that racism is a more widespread social problem than it is. It's important to see the media for what it is: a business—one that aims at increasing views, clicks, and subscriptions. The media has realized that anti-black racism sells, so it highlights anything that can be spun in that direction.

You might object that social media and smartphones have merely made us more aware of the widespread racism that's actually out there. If this were true, then we'd expect Americans in the age of social media to have an accurate perception of the amount of racism in society. That proposition has been tested, and has come back negative. For instance, 54 percent of "very liberal" Americans—the section of the population most active on social media—believe that over one thousand unarmed black men were killed by the cops in 2019. The real number was twelve. Social media isn't educating us. It's miseducating us.

RACIAL TALK MAKES RACIST THOUGHT

Many would-be anti-racists think that we should talk more about race. They believe that talking about race more will help eliminate racism. But why?

It's true that constantly talking about race increases the level of people's racial awareness—it puts race and racism top of mind. But does it follow that if race is top of mind, then racist attitudes and actions are less likely to occur? Why assume that if you increase the number of thoughts people have about race you'll thereby decrease the number of *bad* thoughts they have about race?

The opposing view was suggested by the actor Morgan Freeman in a 2005 interview with Mike Wallace on the CBS program *60 Minutes*:

MIKE WALLACE: Black History Month, you find . . .

MORGAN FREEMAN: Ridiculous.

WALLACE: Why?

FREEMAN: You're going to relegate my history to a month?

WALLACE: Come on.

FREEMAN: What do you do with yours? Which month is White History Month? Come on, tell me.

WALLACE: I'm Jewish.

FREEMAN: OK. Which month is Jewish History Month?

WALLACE: There isn't one.

FREEMAN: Why not? Do you want one?

WALLACE: No, no.

FREEMAN: I don't either. I don't want a Black History Month. Black history is American history.

WALLACE: How are we going to get rid of racism until . . .

FREEMAN: Stop talking about it. I'm going to stop calling
you a white man. And I'm going to ask you to stop calling
me a black man.

Freeman suggested that the way to reduce racism is not by
talking about race more, but by talking about race less. This is an
important insight that many would-be anti-racists miss.

Let's say you wanted to reduce the amount of hatred between
fans of the New York Yankees and fans of the Boston Red Sox—a
tall order indeed. In order to do this, you come up with a proposal: educate the population about the importance of baseball.
Under this strategy, we would start educating kids about baseball as young as possible. By kindergarten, every child in America
would know the basic rules, the history, and nuances of baseball. Every gym class would be substituted with a baseball game.
Whenever possible, homework and test questions would utilize
examples from baseball.

It's not clear to me that this strategy would decrease the sum
total of hatred between Yankees fans and Red Sox fans. If anything, it seems more likely that it would increase hatred. The
more people there are who care about baseball, and the more
deeply they care about it, the more attached they will likely feel
to their home teams. And the more it will hurt to lose. At the
very least, it is not obvious that raising the salience of baseball
would be the best strategy for reducing inter-team hostility.

The same may be true of race. Perhaps raising the overall
salience of racial identity actually increases interracial tensions.
Perhaps the more frequently we talk about racial identity and the

more we emphasize its importance, the more race becomes a container not just for the good elements of human nature (e.g., empathy, altruism, kindness, understanding) but also for the nasty elements of human nature (e.g., hatred, paranoia, bullying, insecurity). Though it is difficult to prove this claim with data, this hypothesis would certainly be *consistent* with the data shown in this chapter—namely a declining perception of race relations over the same time period as a roughly tenfold increase in media mentions of race.

That's my hypothesis: racial talk makes racist thought. At the very least, it seems at least as likely to be true as the alternative. Based on what evidence do neoracists believe that talking more and more about race will lead to a decrease in racist thoughts and impulses, rather than an increase? This is widely assumed and nowhere justified by evidence. On what basis do they believe that we as a society can drastically increase the total number of race thoughts we have per day but somehow (with surgical precision) increase only the kind of thoughts that are benign?

Let me make one thing clear: I'm strongly in favor of talking about real instances of racial discrimination and real systemic discrimination in institutions. To give one example, a sting operation with trained actors and secret cameras discovered that Long Island real estate agents discriminated against 19 percent of Asian prospective homeowners, 39 percent of Hispanics, and 49 percent of blacks. That's worth talking about. But most mainstream racial talk doesn't deal with actual racism. Most of it aims at stereotyping people of different races—for example, white people as privileged oppressors and black people as hapless victims. And most mainstream racial talk encourages people to identify ever more strongly with a particular racial group.

None of this combats actual racial discrimination. It's easy to see why. We overcome divisions among people not by emphasizing differences but by emphasizing similarities, and race concepts, by their very nature, emphasize differences. Humans are always going to divide themselves into groups. Throughout human history, race concepts have been among the most frequently used tools for doing that. They don't have to be, but if those are the concepts people are most familiar with, then they will be. If we want to combat racism, we need to start talking more about our common humanity—the idea at the heart of the abolition and civil rights movement.

5

The Neoracist Narrative

Most readers will agree that it is dangerous to understate the amount of racism in society. If the problem of racism is bigger than we assume, then we cannot hope to address it effectively. Moreover, it does people of color no good to march into educational and workplace environments naive to the racism they're likely to face.

In light of this fact, why not err on the side of overestimating racism? When in doubt, shouldn't we assume that there's *more* racism in society, rather than less?

The short answer is no. It's important to be accurate, precise, and rational with regard to the scope and power of racism against people of color today. But rather than give a series of arguments to this effect, I want to tell a quick story.

My grandfather, Warren Hughes, was born to a poor family in segregated Washington, DC, in 1933. After receiving a degree in engineering from Ohio State University (one of the few blacks to receive such a degree in those days) and serving in the Korean War, he secured a job as an engineer with General Electric. For his ninetieth birthday, he wrote a short memoir, which included his reflections on navigating General Electric as a black man:

> It was in September 1959 that I got a more permanent position in Cincinnati, Ohio, working for General Electric. That's when I began to recognize that the outlook for a Black engineer in those days was different from that of a White engineer. I was told, in fact, that General Electric allows you to advance two ways: one is the management way up, and the other is technical. In other words, you can make the same amount of money by being a manager or by being very good technically. I was told by a well meaning White engineer that I should not strive to go the management route because the White guys who were the technical experts (welders and welding specialists) would not work for a Black manager. What I could do was become the best in my class and a technical expert. Well, at the time, that was not so much of a problem for me.
>
> So, I was in regular engineering status for about ten years, but that was because I accepted what my White colleague had said, and I knew he was well meaning. Well, then, times were changing, and I found out that he was as wrong as he could be. A vacancy came up in my department, and they hired a manager and placed him over me, but I kept my position. However, that manager moved on to greener

pastures, so the boss of the section was looking for someone to take his job. When I realized that the manager had been doing just the same kind of thing I had always been doing and that the boss was going to fill the vacancy with a White guy who didn't even have my experience and who wasn't even there half the time, I decided to go ahead and talk to my boss about the position. My boss was genuinely shocked that I asked because I had never given him the impression that I was interested in management.

Well, he gave me the job immediately. Interestingly, I found that the White guys—yes, they were all specialists in their fields—liked working for me. In fact, I had no problems whatsoever with them.

My grandfather went on to have a stellar career, eventually reaching the executive level by the 1980s. Had he listened to his well-meaning white colleague who overstated the amount of racism at General Electric, he would never have sought out the management position that led him to greater success. He may have lived his whole life telling himself that racism had held him back—and his background would have given him ample reason to believe this story. Just as there is a danger in understating the amount of racism in society, there is a less obvious (and therefore more pernicious) danger in overstating it. To exaggerate the extent of anti-black racism in society is to reduce every black person's incentive to reach higher.

In this chapter, we will attempt to see racism for what it is—without either overstating or understating its scope and power.

We will also attempt to see neoracism for what it is: a dangerous ideology that does not make contact with reality. Neoracism takes grains of truth and builds them into a powerfully seductive narrative.

The Neoracist Narrative: White people have always had power in society—power that they've used to create systems like slavery and Jim Crow that oppress people of color. Even though these systems were destroyed, American society has made little or no progress redressing the wrongs that white people have inflicted on people of color in the past and continue to inflict on people of color in the present. People of color continue suffering from the inertia of white supremacist systems, and they continue experiencing the pain and trauma that was inflicted on their enslaved ancestors. All around us, policies and institutions give rise to racial disparities—differences in outcomes between white people and people of color. In case after case, we see people of color receiving a smaller share of society's benefits and a larger share of society's harms. Wherever racial disparities exist, racism—past and present—is the cause. To make matters worse, white Americans are largely oblivious to the racism they perpetuate. They are blind to the plight of people of color and deaf to their pleas. And no wonder: there is no real way for them to understand the many ways in which people of color are made to suffer. Even the least-educated person of color has a better understanding of race and racism than the best-educated white person. Justice demands that we work to undo the wrongs of the past. It demands that we implement policies that rebalance the way resources are distributed. Wherever possible, we need to give people of color preferential treatment. This is the only way for our society to move beyond its checkered racial past and defeat white supremacy.

As seductive as this narrative is, it depends on several harmful myths and fallacies built into neoracist ideology. As I go through them, keep my grandfather's story, and the lesson it embodies, in mind: comforting falsehoods help no one, least of all people of color. These falsehoods include the following:

The Disparity Fallacy: Racial disparities provide direct evidence of systemic racism.

The Myth of Undoing the Past: New acts of racial discrimination can undo the effects of past racial discrimination.

The Myth of No Progress: American society has made little or no progress combating racism against people of color since the civil rights movement.

The Myth of Inherited Trauma: Black people who are alive today inherit the trauma that was inflicted on their enslaved ancestors.

The Myth of Superior Knowledge: The knowledge that people of color have about racism is superior to any knowledge about racism that a white person could have.

The Racial Ad Hominem: You can dismiss any claims about race and racism that white people make simply because they are white.

The Myth of Black Weakness: White people have power in society, but black people don't.

THE DISPARITY FALLACY

We've seen that neoracists use the concept of systemic racism to absolve themselves of any responsibility for proving accusations of racism. As Ibram X. Kendi puts it, "When I see racial disparities, I see racism." To make these accusations, they instead follow a pattern of faulty reasoning: They start with a racial disparity in some domain. They then leap to the conclusion that this disparity must be due to racism. When they can't pinpoint a source for the discrimination, they claim that the racism is systemic—that it's not due to any individual or group of individuals but is instead "baked into" the system. I call this faulty pattern of reasoning the Disparity Fallacy.

The logic behind the Disparity Fallacy resembles the logic behind tree-ring climatology. Climatologists can't directly measure the temperature of the earth a thousand years ago. But they can measure it indirectly by measuring the rings inside a thousand-year-old tree: the wider the ring, the warmer the climate that year. Similarly, neoracists can't directly measure the amount of systemic racism in society. But they believe they can measure it indirectly by treating racial disparities like tree rings—the wider the disparity, the more systemic racism exists.

No one can deny that racism exists in both overt and subtle forms. What neoracists assert, however, goes beyond this claim.

Neoracists believe that there would be no racial disparities, or at least no large ones, in a fair society. Kendi puts it this way:

> If Black people make up 13.2 percent of the US population, then Black people should make up somewhere close to 13 percent of the Americans killed by the police, somewhere close to 13 percent of Americans sitting in prisons, somewhere close to owning 13 percent of US wealth.

The Disparity Fallacy assumes, in other words, that all disparities are malignant. But disparities are like tumors; they can be malignant or they can be benign. *Malignant disparities* are those caused by discrimination—or otherwise arrived at through an unfair process. *Benign disparities* arise naturally because of cultural and demographic differences between groups.

Indeed, as we will see, many disparities are benign—so benign that we do not even realize they are there. Yet the Disparity Fallacy collapses these two categories and considers all disparities to be malignant—prescribing invasive procedures to remove them even when such procedures do more harm than good. Let's examine the reasons why the Disparity Fallacy is wrong and see the harm that it causes.

Demographic Differences

Demographic differences alone can create benign disparities between racial and ethnic groups. A simple example is age. While the median white American is forty-three years old, the median black American is only thirty-three years old. Because human beings generally earn more money and commit less crime as they age (in addition to a host of other changes), comparing the outcomes of whites and blacks without controlling for age exaggerates the disparity between them. Comparing Hispanics and whites who are separated by a fourteen-year age gap is even more misleading. Yet this is routine practice in newspaper articles and even academic papers.

Geographical differences can create benign disparities as well. A recent analysis by *The Washington Post*, for instance, found that Americans from the South had worse credit scores than Americans in any other part of the nation. The researchers assumed that this was because the South was disproportionately black. But when they checked, they found that the blackest areas of the South had the same low credit scores as the least-black areas of the South. Why geographical differences so often cause benign disparities is a complex question. But part of that answer pertains to the crux of the issue with the Disparity Fallacy: culture.

The Power of Culture

Even when we hold measurable variables like age and geography constant, there is the problem of culture. It's common knowledge that cultures differ from one another. What else could the "multi" in "multicultural" mean? What else could we be referring to when we promote "cultural diversity"? Moreover, culture matters a great deal in shaping who we become. Anyone who isn't a genetic determinist—in addition to anyone who has decried rape culture, gun culture, or consumer culture—understands that culture matters.

Put those two beliefs together—cultures differ and culture matters—and you should arrive at the conclusion that differences between cultures matter. Yet in the context of racial inequality, the very mention of culture remains off-limits, so much so that Harvard professor Orlando Patterson once joked about a fellow sociologist refusing to utter the "C-word."

The neoracist opposition to cultural explanations of disparity will seem ironic to anyone who knows the history of such explanations. Cultural explanations of racial disparity have played an important role in combating racism. In the early twentieth century, for instance, anthropologists like Franz Boas and Ruth Benedict combated Nazi theories of race supremacy by locating the source of group differences in culture instead of genetics. Nurture explained those differences, they said, not nature. Culture is learned and malleable rather than innate and fixed. So cultural explanations provided powerful refutations of claims that some races were naturally and immutably superior to others.

The idea that appeals to culture are racist is not only historically ignorant but also conceptually confused. Race and culture, though often correlated, are separate concepts. For instance, two groups can possess different cultures while belonging to the same race. Consider the cultural differences between blacks of American descent and blacks of Caribbean descent. Studying both groups in New York City, Columbia sociologist Van Tran found that, compared with American blacks, Caribbean blacks were more likely to express disapproval of drug use, less likely to be connected to their neighborhood social network, and more likely to condone strict parenting—up to and including corporal punishment. Caribbean blacks also earned more money than American blacks, were more likely to be employed, and less likely to be teenage mothers—despite living in equally segregated neighborhoods. The point here is not to weigh the costs and benefits of different cultural attitudes, much less to pass moral judgment on any particular group. The point is to underscore the distinction between race and culture. How could it be racist to cite culture as the explanation for a disparity between ethnic groups of the same race?

Different Cultures Yield Different Outcomes

Cultural differences are especially powerful at shaping outcomes. Culture mediates what people care about and hence what kinds of ends they're motivated to pursue.

Why are approximately 80 percent of the world's pianists Chinese, when the Chinese comprise only 18 percent of the world population? Well, there's no gene for playing the piano, and there is no systemic bias preventing non-Chinese people from playing the piano. The answer has to do with culture: mastery of classical concert piano is highly valued in modern Chinese culture. A higher proportion of parents start their kids on piano at a young age, and those kids are reinforced by the fact that many of their friends play piano as well. That fact alone is enough to create a benign disparity in which Chinese people are "overrepresented" at the highest levels of piano playing.

Why are there many chess grand masters from Kazakhstan

and Uzbekistan but none from Japan? (GM Hikaru Nakamura is considered to be an American grand master, though he was born in Japan.) Again the answer is cultural: In Japanese culture, people tend not to play Western chess but instead play games like Go or Shogi. Kazakhstan and Uzbekistan, on the other hand, were part of the Soviet Union in the twentieth century—the most chess-obsessed culture in the world at the time. Again, this cultural fact alone is enough to produce a large but benign disparity in which some groups are "overrepresented" and others are "underrepresented."

The more I have studied disparities in multicultural societies, the more I have found the language of "overrepresentation" and "underrepresentation" to be fundamentally misleading. These words assume that there is something normal or "to be expected" about seeing different ethnic groups represented at precisely their share of the total population in every domain, statistic, and occupation, when in fact nothing is more normal than for different subcultures to specialize in particular sectors and occupations and experience very different group-wide statistics as a result. The vast majority of such disparities are not plausibly explained by bigotry, systemic racism, or unfairness but by demographic and cultural differences between the groups in question at a particular time.

Here are some examples of large disparities that cannot be explained in terms of racism for or against either group of people:

- In 1950, the persecuted Japanese minority in California had more years of education in America, on average, than whites.

- In the 1990s, over four-fifths of doughnut shops in California were owned by people of Cambodian descent.

- In the mid-twentieth century, the Puerto Rican minority in St. Croix, at one-quarter of the population, owned and operated over half of the businesses on the island.

- In the early twentieth century, black Caribbeans owned the majority of businesses in Harlem despite being a minority relative to the black American population.

- In 1920, Jews accounted for half the lawyers and three-fifths of the doctors in Hungary, at 6 percent of the total population.

- During World War I, black soldiers from northern states scored higher than white soldiers from southern states in tests of mental ability.

- In 1998, Americans raised in Jewish households had almost six times the median net worth of Americans raised in conservative Protestant households.

- A study of net worth in Boston found that black Caribbeans had a median net worth of $12,000, while black Americans, Puerto Ricans, and Dominicans had median net worths close to zero.

Again, the point of these examples isn't to pass judgment on any particular group. The point is instead to illustrate how common it is to see large disparities that cannot be explained by racism.

The Importance of Process

Calling an outcome unfair requires showing that the process that yielded the outcome was unfair. Yet neoracists often label outcomes unfair without examining the processes that produce them.

Think about how this principle applies in a domain like professional sports. Is anyone suspicious about 75 percent of NBA players being black? Does anyone accuse the NBA recruitment system of anti-white racism? No. Most people feel confident that the system is not racist. They feel confident that the system is broadly meritocratic. If it turns out that most of the best players are black, then so be it. People become suspicious of the results only when they suspect that there's unfairness in the process that's producing those results.

Imagine that we instituted a "racial equity" policy in the NBA, whereby the NBA had to be 13 percent black. We could achieve the racial equity for which people like Kendi advocate, but we would clearly have to discriminate against individual black players to get there. Racist processes can produce equal outcomes, and colorblind processes can produce unequal outcomes. In other words, there is a perfect dissociation between the fairness of a process and the equality of the result. So if you're going to accuse a system of being unfair, it's not enough simply to look at the outcomes. You need to look at the process that produced them.

Accusing the system of being unfair requires showing one of two things: either the people involved in the process acted unfairly or else the policies, rules, or procedures they're using are structured in a way that produces unfair results. This is what a responsible accusation of systemic racism would have to show. We've seen, however, that neoracists aren't interested in fixing the systems we have. That's why they resort to the Disparity Fallacy. They're not interested in identifying and fixing real sources of unfairness.

Systemic Racism

So far I've argued that there is such a thing as a benign disparity— and that the mere existence of a disparity does not tell you whether it is benign (not caused by racism) or malignant (caused by racism). In order to determine whether a disparity is benign or malignant, you have to look closely at the process that produced it.

The best way to do this is via experiment. The past two decades have seen a surge of interest in measuring racial discrimination in the labor market. The gold standard for studies in this area is "callback" studies. They work like this: Researchers create a set of identical résumés, but give one a "black-sounding" name, another a "white-sounding" name, another a "Chinese-sounding" name, and so on. They send out thousands of these applications for real job openings and measure the racial disparity in callbacks received. (See Appendix D for a discussion of why this way of measuring racism is superior to others.)

These studies have found a large and clear bias against minorities in the labor market. The largest meta-analysis of such studies to date analyzed 306 experiments that represented a combined 965,000 fake applications for real jobs. The results found that black job applicants were 32 percent less likely to receive a reply, Arabs were 41 percent less likely to receive a reply, Indians and South Asians were 30 percent less likely to receive a reply, and East Asians were 27 percent less likely to receive a reply.

On its face, this might seem to be strong evidence that black-white disparities in income, for instance, are malignant rather than benign. But that's the wrong conclusion to draw. We must consider the fact that ethnic groups who face the same level of labor market discrimination nevertheless occupy opposite ends of the socioeconomic spectrum. Indian Americans, for instance, are the top-earning ethnic group in the nation—earning $1.50 for every dollar earned by a white American. At the same time, Bengali Americans—who belong to the same "race" as Indian Americans—earn $0.65 on the median white dollar. Chinese Americans earn $1.18 on the median white dollar, while Hmong Americans earn just $0.52.

Most would-be employers could not tell the difference between a person of Hmong descent and a person of Chinese descent. Nor could most employers tell the difference between an Indian and a Bengali. Certainly, differences in the amount of discrimination faced cannot explain the wide income gaps between these groups. If discrimination were the main determinant of income, then we would expect to see similar levels of income from groups that face similar levels of discrimination. Instead we see groups that face lots of labor market discrimination scattered all over the income spectrum, from the very top to the very bottom.

This suggests that the variable of racial discrimination has a relatively small effect on average income—that is, relative to the combined effect of all the other factors that determine income, such as a person's overall skills, knowledge, abilities, and social network. The takeaway from the callback research therefore is this: minorities face a significant amount of unfair discrimination in the labor market, but the effect of that discrimination on their income is surprisingly small.

None of this implies that racial discrimination doesn't matter ethically, socially, and psychologically. There are still good reasons to care about fighting discrimination, and in chapter six, I will suggest some ways of doing that. What I am arguing here is that current racial discrimination is not a significant cause of current racial disparities in income.

Creating Racist Processes

The Disparity Fallacy is a mistake in reasoning. It's lured so many people into making false or unsubstantiated claims. That's bad in itself. But the damage it's done goes beyond that. The Disparity Fallacy has made our society more racist.

The Disparity Fallacy has inspired people to introduce race into processes that originally had nothing to do with race, transforming race-neutral processes into racist ones. For instance, since 1991 air traffic controllers have been hired based upon a rigorous, merit-based process. If you earned a degree from an FAA Collegiate Training Initiative (CTI) school and scored high enough on an eight-hour exam called the AT-SAT, you were given hiring preference. And even if you clear those hurdles, you still have months of training at the FAA academy and years of on-the-job training—hurdles that weed out over half of applicants.

As a retired air traffic controller put it, "This profession isn't like any other. Errors are deadly and perfection is the standard."

That was the hiring process until the Obama administration decided that there were too few racial minorities among air traffic controllers. His administration changed the rules to make going to a CTI school and passing the AT-SAT exam irrelevant—replacing them with a mysterious biographical questionnaire (BQ) that asked questions like, "What has been the major cause of your failures?"—questions that were subtly designed to favor non-white applicants. Thousands of people who had already gotten the right degree and aced the difficult exam were now told that those hard-won achievements meant nothing, and that they would have to reapply by taking the BQ. A class action suit on their behalf is ongoing.

THE MYTH OF UNDOING THE PAST

You might be thinking, "Coleman, this whole time you've been criticizing self-proclaimed 'anti-racists' like Kendi and DiAngelo. But you're not taking into account what motivates them: the need to right past wrongs. White people in America oppressed black people for a long time. It's now time to make up for that history of oppression. Our society as a whole needs to start boosting black people up and, if necessary, to start pushing white people down. Only in that way can we repair the history of injustice that includes the horrors of slavery and Jim Crow."

This objection assumes that the way to combat injustice is

with more injustice. But that is false. Cycles of ethnic violence around the world show us again and again that a society doesn't overcome injustice by creating new forms of it. They show us that the law of retaliation, the principle of taking an eye for an eye, is a simplistic and outmoded way to think of justice, one that leads to interminable hatred generation after generation.

Yet this perverse conception of justice lies at the heart of neoracist ideology. Think again of Kendi's words:

> The only remedy to racist discrimination is antiracist discrimination. The only remedy to past discrimination is present discrimination. The only remedy to present discrimination is future discrimination.

Kendi explicitly endorses the logic of taking an eye for an eye. He supposes that the way to remedy a harm is by imposing an equal and opposite harm—that the way to remedy one kind of injustice is by replacing it with another kind of injustice: if I strike you, you strike me; if I steal from you, you steal from me; if I kill your child, you kill mine.

Human history shows us how wrongheaded the neoracist conception of justice is. It shows us that taking an eye for an eye doesn't stop injustice; it instead participates in it. It creates new injustices in a misguided effort to remedy old ones. It then demands that those new injustices be remedied by yet newer injustices in the future. The neoracist logic of retaliation will lead inevitably to a cycle of wrongful discrimination that never ends.

Numerous historical examples could be given. But consider one from a context that is foreign to most Western readers: The conflict between the Han and the Manchus in China. When the Manchu conquered China in the seventeenth century, they relegated the Han majority to second-class status—going so far as to force all Han males, on pain of death, to wear the traditional Manchu hairstyle consisting of a single long braid. Yet as the Qing dynasty progressed, anti-Manchu sentiment gained power. Such sentiments reached violent levels during the Taiping rebellion, when a coalition led by a Han general prosecuted a mass killing of Manchus, whom they considered a "barbarian" race. By the end of the 1911 revolution—in which rebels slaughtered untold Manchu civilians and enslaved many women—the power reversal was complete: after centuries of dominating the Hans, the Manchu "quickly fell to the lowest stratum of Chinese society," in the words of one historian. They were even forced to cut their braids. Is there any doubt that the subjugation of the Manchus added to the sum total of suffering in the world, rather than canceling out the suffering of previous generations of Han?

I've intentionally given an example from a context foreign to most of my readers because this dynamic can be easier to see through a more detached lens. But let's apply it to an American context. Discriminating against white people in the present doesn't erase the injustice of discrimination against black people in the past. It doesn't decrease the sum total of injustice in the world. Neoracists often act as if various kinds of discrimination move a placeholder on a justice number line. Acts of anti-black discrimination in the past moved the placeholder toward the negative end of the number line: −2 points for this act, −5 points for that act, and so on. Neoracists imagine that we need to move the placeholder back to zero, and that the way to do that is by engaging in acts of anti-white discrimination today—acts of retribution that move the placeholder farther up the number line: +2 points for this act of anti-white discrimination, +5 for that act, and so on.

But that's not how justice works. Any act of injustice adds to the sum total of injustice in the world. Anti-black discrimination in the past added to the sum total of injustice in the world, and anti-white discrimination in the present adds yet more injustice to the world—without canceling the effects of past discrimination against blacks.

If my grandfather was discriminated against for a job in the 1950s, it doesn't undo the effects of that discrimination to discriminate unfairly against a white job applicant today. Doing that won't compensate my grandfather for his loss of income, or for his pain, anger, or humiliation at having been unjustly discriminated against. None of that is erased by discriminating against a white job applicant in the present—or by giving me a leg up. Rather, the present act of discrimination simply adds a new injustice to the growing sum of injustices, past and present.

Compensating my grandfather directly might go some way toward redressing the injustice he's suffered. That's why I have always supported reparations paid to specific living victims of government abuses. But a new act of discrimination aimed at some other person—that wouldn't even provide compensation. It would just add to the tally of wrongs that people have perpetrated against one another throughout history.

The neoracist pretense of undoing past wrongs reflects a desire for something like what Thomas Sowell calls "cosmic justice"—the kind of resolution of injustice that could be achieved only by an omnipotent being. But a desire for divine recompense is a recipe for bad policy—one that tries to achieve the impossible. Striving for the common good has to take place in the realm of what's possible. We can end current systems of injustice. We can compensate living victims of injustice. But we're not omnipotent. We can't undo the past or compensate the dead. Their value to us in the present consists in the lessons they have to teach us about how to create a more just society for the future.

If our desire to undo the effects of the past provides a legitimate rationale for discrimination in the present, where does it end? If, as Kendi argues, "the only remedy to past discrimination is present discrimination," why not apply this logic even more widely than we already have? Why not, for instance, give black Americans 1.5 votes per person? By Kendi's logic, this would be a straightforward way to redress the long and well-documented history of black Americans being denied the right to vote.

I could even imagine a neoracist ideologue arguing for this policy in impassioned tones: *"You mean after hundreds of years of being denied the right to vote and suffering and dying due to our lack of political power, you're not willing to balance the scales by giving black Americans a measly 1.5 votes per person? What about 1.1? It's not like this would destroy the white American population. They'll be fine. They've always had more political power than us. Are you not willing to do anything concrete to redress the history of voting discrimination in this country? Do you not care at all about the history of racism?"*

If you accept the argument that redressing past discrimination justifies present discrimination—one of the most common arguments in support of race-based affirmative action and similar policies—then what would stop you from supporting this race-based voting policy, other than realpolitik? What, in other words, is the internal limiting principle on the idea of undoing past racism? I have never heard one articulated, and I worry that there is no such limiting principle.

What the lessons of past discrimination teach us is that the way to move a society beyond a history of bigotry is not with more bigotry. It's not by sanctioning new forms of bigotry that reverse the forms of bigotry that have been socially sanctioned in the past, or by allowing different forms of bigotry to take turns ruining the lives of one group of people after another.

The way for a society to move beyond a history of bigotry is instead to deny latitude for any kind of bigotry to operate in society. It's to stigmatize all forms of bigotry and to emphasize our common humanity. Leaders of the civil rights movement embraced our common humanity and opposed any kind of racial discrimination. They saw clearly that the remedy for discrimination was not more discrimination; it was instead putting an end to discrimination once and for all.

THE MYTH OF NO PROGRESS

Neoracism relies on another myth, which I call the Myth of No Progress. It claims that American society has made little or no progress combating racism against people of color since the civil rights movement. The author Michelle Alexander, for instance, claims that "African Americans, as a group, are no better off than they were in 1968 in many respects. In fact, to some extent, they are worse off."

But neoracists are wrong. There are numerous indications

that American society has made tremendous progress since the civil rights movement.

Indicators of Real Progress

The past sixty years have witnessed unprecedented progress in combating racism against people of color—progress that's evident in numerous ways.

Consider, for instance, attitudes toward interracial marriage. In 1958, when Gallup first began asking Americans whether they approved of marriage between whites and non-whites, only 4 percent stated approval. That number steadily increased, and in 2021 it was at 94 percent.

Consider likewise that the number of black Americans holding positions of leadership in society has gone up. In 1965 only five members of the US House of Representatives were black. By 2021 that number reached 57. Similarly, in 1958 only 38 percent of Americans said they'd support a well-qualified black candidate for president. That number steadily increased, and in 2019 it stood at 96 percent.

On the flip side, consider incarceration rates. Since 2001, the national incarceration rate for black men ages eighteen to twenty-nine has gone down by more than half. The great incarceration decline for black youth has been matched by a decline in teenage motherhood. Between 2001 and 2017, the birth rate for black women ages fifteen to nineteen declined by 63 percent. In fact, the black teenage birth rate in 2017 was lower than the *white* teenage rate as recently as 2002.

Neoracists claim that black Americans in general are less

likely than white Americans to go from poverty to wealth in the course of their lifetimes. But this generalization is false. The Federal Reserve recently reported that over 60 percent of blacks at every level of educational attainment say they're doing better financially than their parents—a higher percentage than either whites or Hispanics. In a landmark study of social mobility, economist Raj Chetty discovered that there is no racial gap in upward mobility for women. In other words, black girls and white girls born into households of equal income will grow up to make, on average, the same amount of money.

One of the more interesting indicators of declining racism comes from research on the phenomenon of "passing." Human beings are amazingly intuitive calculators of the costs and benefits of identifying one way as opposed to another. And history shows that, if able, we are willing to identify differently in response to social and economic incentive structures. In the nineteenth and early twentieth centuries, for example, light-skinned black Americans would often "pass" for white in order to escape the racist stranglehold of Jim Crow. Rigorous estimates suggest that an astounding 17 percent of black American men at some point in their lives began living socially as white between the years 1880 and 1940. This phenomenon is virtually unheard of today. By and large, light-skinned black people do not try to pass for white in order to escape racism. Indeed, the one famous case of "passing" in our age has been Rachel Dolezal, a white woman who tried to pass for black.

That said, there is evidence that a small minority of people with mixed ancestry still change their self-identified race in response to incentives today. A group of MIT researchers used state-level affirmative action bans in various states during the 1990s and 2000s as natural experiments to see if people who had an incentive to change their self-identified race would do so on the census. They found that 15 percent of young people who identified as mixed-race blacks *before* the bans stopped identifying as black *after* the bans. They found the opposite trend for young Asian Americans, who suffer discrimination under affirmative action: mixed-race Asians were 15 percent *more* likely to identify as Asian after an affirmative action ban.

To be clear, I don't think we should interpret modern race-switching as equivalent to race-switching under Jim Crow. For one thing, the numbers are much smaller and the stakes much lower. So, broadly, it is consistent with the long-run decline of societal racism. The likeliest explanation of race-switching today is that a small minority of mixed-race people pay close attention to policy changes that will give them marginal advantages—and strategically identify on government forms in response to those policies—whether or not those identities reflect their everyday social identity. There may be a kind of dishonesty in this, but it is a dishonesty that is encouraged by our regime of race-based policies.

The Decline of White Supremacy

Yet another indicator of the progress American society has made in combating anti-black racism is the overall decline of white supremacy and white supremacist organizations. When many people think of white supremacy in the United States today, they think of a single event: the 2017 Unite the Right rally in Charlottesville, Virginia. As many as five hundred participants arrived to protest the proposed removal of a statue of General Robert E. Lee from a Charlottesville public park, but they were met by more than a thousand counterprotesters. It was at this infamous event that a white supremacist named James Alex Fields Jr. rammed his car into a crowd of counterprotesters. Thirty-five people were injured, and one of them, the civil rights activist Heather Heyer, was killed. Fields was tried and convicted of first-degree murder, and is currently serving a life sentence.

The violence perpetrated by Fields was utterly reprehensible. We are right to be shocked and repulsed by it. But how much does that event represent the current state of white supremacy in the United States?

A year later, in 2018, there was a second Unite the Right rally in Washington, DC. This time, only twenty-five white supremacists showed up. They were met by thousands of counterprotesters, along with hundreds of police officers. One counterprotester, a podcaster named Bridget Todd, commented, "They're terrible at organizing . . . I had more people at my niece's baby shower than this." A few hours in, it started raining. The white supremacists went home. The counterprotesters didn't even notice.

This story is an apt metaphor for white supremacy in our time—an increasingly fringe and cringe-worthy movement that's been declining for decades. According to the Anti-Defamation League, the Ku Klux Klan had only about 3,000 members nationwide in 2016 (compared to more than a million a century ago). For comparison: the Flat Earth Society has boasted a membership of 3,500 people.

But the declining number of white supremacists is only part of the story. The social power of white supremacists is even

smaller than their meager numbers would suggest. White supremacist ideas have been widely shamed and tabooed. Few
people are even tempted to defend them. Yet neoracists continue
depicting white supremacy as a powerful movement that threat-
ens our democracy.

Mainstream American society isn't morally confused about
white supremacy; it's an ideology that most Americans reject on
moral grounds. By contrast, many Americans are morally confused about neoracism. They're fooled by the self-proclaimed
"anti-racist" label that neoracists have adopted. That moral confusion makes neoracism a more dangerous threat to the dream.

White supremacy is a wolf in wolf's clothing. It has long
been exposed for what it is, and people aren't fooled by it. Neoracism, by contrast, is a wolf in sheep's clothing. It uses the guise
of anti-racism as a lure to garner support from well-intentioned—
if misguided—people who want to support the cause of anti-
racism but are no longer sure how.

The Unforgiveness Treadmill

Another part of the Myth of No Progress is the persistent denial
that America has done anything significant to acknowledge and
atone for its past. Neoracists are fond of claiming that Americans
are by and large ignorant about slavery, unwilling to acknowledge its legacy, and resistant to any efforts at compensating black
Americans descended from slaves.

This characterization of America was no doubt true up until
the 1960s—and remained true in some pockets of America for
decades after that. But mainstream American culture has changed

in the past sixty years. Much has been done in the spirit of reparations—both in our public policy and in our culture at large. Yet neoracists either take these efforts for granted or else conveniently forget them. It's only this practiced amnesia that emboldens neoracists to claim that America hasn't made serious efforts to atone for its past.

What are those efforts? Let's start with some important symbolic gestures on the part of governments. The US House of Representatives formally apologized for slavery in 2008; the Senate did the same in 2009—an event preceded four years earlier by an official apology for lynching. Likewise, at the state level, Virginia issued a formal apology for slavery in 2007. Since then eight other states have followed suit.

Other important symbolic gestures include establishing federal holidays that honor the historic struggle against racism in our country. Two of our eleven official federal holidays are dedicated to different aspects of the black freedom struggle: one celebrates Martin Luther King Jr., our national hero and martyr in the fight against Jim Crow; the other, Juneteenth, celebrates the emancipation of slaves following the Civil War. Think likewise of the creation of Black History Month—something celebrated voluntarily by schools, corporations, and public institutions all over the nation.

The nation's capital hosts a magnificent Smithsonian museum dedicated to the history and culture of African Americans—including an extensive exhibit on slavery and the middle passage. During its construction, public enthusiasm for the museum was so high that it outraised its fundraising goal by over $100 million. When it opened in 2016, attendance was much higher than expected, and the average museumgoer spent twice as long per visit as officials had anticipated. What's more, museumgoers were spending so much time in the exhibit on slavery and the middle passage that officials had to limit the number of people who could enter in order to avoid dangerous overcrowding. None of this paints a picture of a general public, or a government, that is resistant to historical soul-searching.

As for concrete policies that have been implemented in the spirit of reparations, affirmative action in hiring and college admissions certainly qualifies. These days, affirmative action is typically justified in the name of promoting diversity. But when the policy first emerged in the late 1960s and early '70s, it was typically justified in the name of compensating black Americans for past racism. In fact, in those days the cluster of policies we now call "affirmative action" often went by a different name: "compensatory justice."

Several years ago, I had a conversation with a journalist from a major online magazine about reparations for slavery. She was writing an article about the reparations debate, and she wanted to include my perspective as an opponent of the idea. At one point, she asked if I would at least support the creation of a documentary or miniseries about slavery—a major film event that the entire nation would tune in to. She suggested that this would go a long way toward increasing awareness of slavery's legacy in mainstream American culture. "Absolutely, I'd support that," I told her, "but isn't that what *Roots* was?" She'd never heard of *Roots*. I explained that *Roots* was a TV series that aired on CBS in the 1970s that followed the story of a boy named Kunta Kinte, who was kidnapped off the shores of West Africa by European slave traders, sold into slavery in Virginia, and punished brutally when he tried to escape.

At first, it surprised me that a journalist writing about slavery at a major online magazine had not heard of *Roots*. More Americans watched *Roots* in 1977 than watched the Super Bowl. It shattered every previous record for American television viewership, and few shows in the past four decades have even approached it. Yet *Roots* is barely mentioned in elite media nowadays.

It is not that these apologies, symbolic gestures, and policies never happened. It is that they have been taken for granted and forgotten. It isn't that gestures of regret haven't been made. The problem is that there is a principled refusal by the thought leaders of neoracism to acknowledge them. As a result, the general public is unaware of just how much has been done in the spirit of reparations, much like the journalist who didn't know what *Roots* was.

To this day, it remains a talking point among media pundits that America has "never" issued a formal apology for slavery. NBC News, for instance, released an opinion in 2019 titled, "Congress Must Officially Apologize for Slavery before America Can Think about Reparations." The writers took issue with the fact that the apologies already made by both houses of Congress in 2008 and 2009 were issued independently, rather than as a joint resolution—as if this technicality were the crux of the issue.

We must realize that a game is being played here. Normally when someone demands an apology, they actually want one. But sometimes they don't. Sometimes, the ability to continue demanding the apology is worth more than the apology itself. Sometimes the debt is worth more unpaid than paid. For neoracists, the social and political power that stems from the perception that they are still "owed" something is far more valuable than anything they would get from another national apology or an actual program of national reparations. This is why every new apology, program, or holiday that they demand is forgotten as soon as it's achieved. We are stuck in a vicious cycle of appeasement by one side and goalpost shifting by the other. It's not clear to me whether neoracists play this game consciously or whether there is self-deception involved. But either way, we are indeed playing a game, and if we don't realize it, then everyone loses.

In July 2020, the editorial board of *USA Today* released an article arguing that Juneteenth should be a federal holiday. They made a strong case but cautioned that achieving it "won't necessarily be easy" to achieve, presumably because of the fierce resistance to soul-searching among Americans. Less than a year later, the nation was celebrating Juneteenth as a federal holiday—the bill breezed through Congress with almost no resistance. A few years from now, no one will even remember that this was once considered an unlikely goal.

Americans, and white Westerners broadly, may be the only population on Earth that feels any noteworthy amount of guilt for the sins of its ancestors. Slavery alone demonstrates the point. Beginning with the conquests of Mohammed, Arabs enslaved as many as fourteen million Africans over a period of about a thousand years. Europeans traded about twelve million African slaves over the course of several centuries.

To get a sense of how little guilt exists in the Arab world, consider the fact that, to this day, a common colloquial word for "black person" is the same as the word for "slave."

Little guilt exists among modern West Africans too, whose

ancestors raided for, kept, and sold slaves. I was once at a dinner with some friends from Ghana and Nigeria. They noted that they were taught all about the slave trade (and African participation in it) in school. I asked, "Is there any guilt among West Africans about capturing, keeping, and then selling other Africans to the Europeans?" "No," they told me, "it's just a neutral fact for us."

The presence of ancestral guilt is a curious sociological fact about Westerners. What marks us apart is not how little we care about our sins, but how much we do.

THE MYTH OF INHERITED TRAUMA

Around the time I enrolled at Columbia University, I encountered a new attitude toward America's history of white supremacy. It consisted first and foremost of acting as if the entire history of American racism had happened to you personally—as if the pain endured by slaves had been passed down from generation to generation, like a genetic illness.

I had grown up feeling *sympathy* for the plight of the slaves. Now I was being told that I could have *empathy* with them—that is, I could feel their pain as if I had experienced it myself. Students would ask, "Don't you believe in inherited trauma?" or "Don't you know about PTSD—Post-Traumatic Slave Disorder?" Sometimes these questions were paired with appeals to epigenetics—a new subfield of biology that, it seemed, might provide the idea of inherited trauma with a scientific basis.

The new attitude I encountered at Columbia represents what I call the Myth of Inherited Trauma. The Myth of Inherited Trauma claims that black people who are alive today inherit the trauma that was inflicted on their enslaved ancestors—that they can actually have a direct first-person experience of the kind of pain and suffering their ancestors endured.

I myself am a descendant of slaves. Like many black Americans, I learned about slavery not just through history textbooks but also through family lore. I remember my grandmother solemnly showing me the names of our ancestors in historical records—not on birth or death certificates but in wills. After all, she explained, they were property. Unlike most black Americans, I have a very well-preserved record of my enslaved ancestors. My father's father, Warren Hughes, traces his ancestry back to Wormley Hughes, a gardener on Thomas Jefferson's Monticello plantation. Because Monticello is of special interest to historians, there is unusually robust evidence of our family's roots.

My childhood attitude toward my ancestry was mixed. On the one hand, the mere fact that the name of a human being could be listed alongside inanimate objects and livestock filled me with sadness and confusion. At the same time, I felt pride that my ancestors had overcome a system as brutal and dehumanizing as slavery. It made the obstacles in my own life seem surmountable by comparison. Whenever I faced challenges, physical or mental, I remembered that my enslaved ancestors had overcome much worse.

When I looked at historical documents about slavery, I felt the enormous weight of tragedy. But I didn't feel that it was *my* tragedy. It was instead a tragedy endured by the enslaved people themselves—a grievance that, despite my ancestral connection to it, didn't belong to me.

Whenever classmates at Columbia would raise the topic of inherited trauma, my response was always the same: I'm a descendant of slaves, but I can't detect an iota of stress or trauma caused by my ancestors being slaves. Whatever traumas I've endured are caused by events that happened in my lifetime.

Why Inherited Trauma Is a Myth

Defenders of the Myth of Inherited Trauma might claim that intergenerational trauma survives in the subconscious, where its effects can't be detected even by those experiencing it. But there are at least two reasons to doubt this claim.

First, only one biological mechanism could plausibly cause inherited trauma: epigenetics—the effect of the environment on genes. But even *The New York Times* has published a summary claiming that there isn't a plausible epigenetic basis for inherited trauma: "The research in epigenetics falls well short of demonstrating that past human cruelties affect our physiology today."

Second, if it were true that people inherited the trauma experienced by their distant ancestors, then not just black Americans but virtually all people would be traumatized. What human alive doesn't have ancestors who suffered trauma?

Think specifically about the trauma of slavery. Slavery has been ubiquitous in the world throughout history. As Orlando Patterson put it in his magisterial study of global slavery:

There is nothing notably peculiar about the institution of slavery. It has existed from before the dawn of human history right down to the twentieth century, in the most primitive human societies and in the most civilized. There is no region on earth that has not at some time harbored the institution. Probably there is no group of people whose ancestors were not at one time slaves or slaveholders.

Only in the last few centuries has prohibiting slavery become the norm for human societies. For most of recorded history, slavery was a fact of life. Indeed, slavery has existed in so many societies dating back thousands of years that it would be easier to compile a list of societies that *didn't* have slaves than a list of those that did.

To be sure, what it means to be a slave has varied greatly in different times and places. Not all slaveholding societies made slavery a lifelong status; nor did all such societies make slavery a heritable condition. What's more, only some slaveholding societies instituted slavery along racial lines. But whatever the differences among the countless slaveholding societies throughout history, what unites them is that there was always suffering associated with being a slave: a loss of freedom, autonomy, and personhood. As Patterson put it, "there is no known slaveholding society where the whip was not considered an indispensable instrument."

If it were true that people inherited the trauma experienced by their distant ancestors, then it's not just black people who'd be suffering from inherited trauma. Virtually all people would be suffering from it. Slavery was so widespread in the human past that if we traced the family tree of almost any person alive today we'd likely find some ancestor on that tree who was enslaved or otherwise traumatized by war and famine. So if inherited trauma lurks in the subconscious of black Americans, it also lurks in the subconscious of many other people. But that conclusion doesn't fit the neoracist agenda.

Though inherited trauma has no scientific basis, we are in danger of making it true through social contagion. We know that the human mind is powerfully suggestible. Many social contagions—from spontaneous outbreaks of hiccups to TikTok-induced Tourette's syndrome—have been documented in recent years. If we allow the Myth of Inherited Trauma to thrive, then we run the risk of creating genuine psychological suffering for black people through the powerful effects of suggestibility and social contagion alone. This is a future we should all want to avoid.

Chronic Victimhood

The Myth of Inherited Trauma hurts black people by encouraging an attitude of perpetual victimhood. Victimhood is supposed to be an acute condition, not a chronic one. Everyone is a victim of something at some point. Whether it's illness, injury, ignorance, or just bad luck, at some point everyone suffers from something that compromises their well-being. But in the best cases, that suffering is temporary—people bounce back from injury, illness, financial trouble, or a job loss. In the best cases, victimhood is an acute condition—something that requires immediate attention and that people quickly move past.

But the Myth of Inherited Trauma changes victimhood from an acute condition to a chronic one. It treats victimhood as if it's a genetic disease—something permanent that cannot be overcome.

Trying to transform victimhood into a chronic condition should strike us as highly counterintuitive. Suppose you had a traumatic experience and went to a therapist for help. A wise therapist wouldn't tell you to accept chronic victim status and abandon all hope of recovery, to surrender your autonomy and think of yourself as forever trapped in your experience of trauma. The wise therapist would instead help you develop strategies for moving past the trauma you'd suffered, empowering you to escape the trauma's gravitational pull by rediscovering your autonomy.

Neoracists promote exactly the opposite of what a wise therapist would. They promote a mindset that treats hardship as something that people are powerless to overcome—a mindset that undermines autonomy and agency.

There's a healthier way of viewing the historical suffering of people of color. I'm grateful to my enslaved ancestors for the hardships they endured and overcame. Their victim status wasn't imagined—it was real. They truly suffered through no fault of their own. But what they suffered doesn't affect me personally. I don't and can't feel their pain. To claim otherwise would be a dishonest bid for sympathy.

What I do feel is gratitude for their courage—gratitude that they were able to stay strong and give me the chance to live a life free of the oppression they suffered. Chronic victimhood is not a workable strategy for living a fulfilling life. Living a fulfilling life requires exercising whatever agency you have. But chronic victimhood undermines that agency. It tries to convince you that you're powerless, that victimhood is something that defines you—something you can never get past.

THE MYTH OF SUPERIOR KNOWLEDGE

Earlier we saw that neoracists are committed to a kind of race supremacy. They believe, whether they state it openly or not, that some races are superior to others. We saw, for instance, that they view people of color as morally superior to white people, and view white people as cold, competent agents of evil.

But neoracists take their race supremacy even further. People of color are not only morally superior, they claim; people of color are epistemically superior as well: they have knowledge of race and racism that is superior to the knowledge that white people have. I call this neoracist claim the Myth of Superior Knowledge.

Neoracists use the Myth of Superior Knowledge to preempt any opposition to what they say. If the knowledge people of color have about race and racism is by definition superior to that of white people, as the myth claims, then anything people of color say about race and racism is *incorrigible*; that is, it can't be corrected by white people. On the neoracist view, a white person trying to correct a black person's claims about race or racism is like an elementary school child trying to correct a physicist's claims about quantum mechanics. Just as the child lacks the relevant knowledge to be able to correct the physicist, neoracists think that white people lack the relevant knowledge to engage in discussions with people of color. As Robin DiAngelo puts it, "if you are white, your opinions on racism are most likely ignorant."

Lived Experience

Neoracists often introduce the Myth of Superior Knowledge through the concept of lived experience. The commonsense idea behind the concept of lived experience is based on two observations.

First, everyone experiences life in a unique way. My experiences are different from yours, and yours are different from the next person's. Even if you and I witness or participate in the same event, the ways that you experience that event are different from the ways I do. You see things with your eyes, hear them with your ears, process them with your mind. And since your eyes, ears, and mind are different from mine, the way I see, hear, or process information differs from the way you do.

Second, not everything that each of us experiences in a given situation gets recorded in a medium that other people can readily understand, such as books, articles, or films. Even though we directly experience something, we don't automatically set about describing or communicating it to other people unless prompted.

The practical upshot of these two observations is that when we're trying to understand something or trying to work together with other people to accomplish a common goal, we need to engage with everyone who has a stake in the matter. They might be seeing, hearing, or understanding something we're not. And what they're seeing, hearing, or understanding might not have been recorded in a medium that we've been able to access without having lived it.

Neoracists take this commonsense idea of lived experience and pervert it in a threefold way. First, they racialize the experiential knowledge that people have. Of course, we all have unique experiential knowledge. But neoracists say that it's not our particular location, abilities, disposition, and background that shape the way we experience things; it's our race.

Second, neoracists take the concept of lived experience seriously only when they're talking about people of color. They argue that being a person of color means having a kind of knowledge that's superior to the knowledge that white people have. But the commonsense idea of lived experience applies to all people equally: the experience of every person is different in some respects from the experience of every other person. If it were true that people of color knew things from their direct experience that white people could never know or understand, then wouldn't it also stand to reason that white people knew a different set of things from their direct experience that people of color could never know or understand? After all, you might argue, people of color don't know what it's like to be white any more than white people know what it's like to be people of color. Neoracists don't give a persuasive account of why this principle doesn't go both ways.

Third, neoracists exaggerate the quality of the knowledge we get from lived experience. We've seen that neoracists claim that the knowledge that people of color have about race and racism is incorrigible. Yet this misunderstands the most fundamental thing that common sense tells us about lived experience—namely, that the experience each of us has is limited.

My experience gives me only a partial understanding of things. When I see something with my eyes, hear it with my ears, understand it with my mind, I see it only in part, hear it only in part, understand it only in part. It's precisely because my experience gives me only partial knowledge that I need to engage with other people—that I need to learn about their experiences. Their experiences give them knowledge that I don't have. Granted, my experiences give me knowledge that they don't have as well. But that's the thing about lived experience: it's just the starting point that each of us has for understanding things. Each of us needs to move past our limited perspective and learn about the lived experiences of others so we can achieve a more complete understanding of the world. We need to accept that no one's lived experience is categorically superior to anyone else's; our experiences are simply different.

It's not surprising that neoracists pervert and racialize the commonsense notion of lived experience. Their aim isn't to engage in honest, open discussion; their aim is instead to stifle opposition. Their perverted use of the concept of lived experience is a tactic to do precisely that. They have other tactics as well.

The Racial Ad Hominem

In May 2012, the *LSE Review of Books* published a review of Thomas Sowell's *Intellectuals and Society*. At one point the review's author, Aidan Byrne, quipped, "Easy for a rich white man to say." The only problem: Thomas Sowell is black.

Byrne's gaffe illustrates a favorite neoracist tactic: Racial Ad Hominem. The ad hominem fallacy is a common error in reasoning. It occurs when someone tries to criticize or dismiss a claim by drawing attention to some trait possessed by the person making the claim. Byrne, for instance, tried to criticize or dismiss Sowell's claims by drawing attention to Sowell's alleged whiteness. The implicit assumption here is that if a white person makes the kinds of claims Sowell does in *Intellectuals and Society*, then we can dismiss those claims as false simply because he's white.

This reasoning is a fallacy because the truth or falsity of a claim doesn't depend on who's making that claim; it depends instead on whether the world is the way the claim says it is. It's not false that $2 + 2 = 4$ simply because a white person claims that $2 + 2 = 4$, nor would it be true that $2 + 2 = 5$ if a black person were to claim it so. The statement $2 + 2 = 4$ is true if and only if it really is the case that $2 + 2 = 4$. It doesn't matter who says it. Similarly, it doesn't matter if Sowell is white or black. His statements are true if and only if things really are the way he says they are. Falsifying his statements requires showing that things really aren't the way he describes. It isn't simply a matter of accusing him of being white.

The Racial Ad Hominem is a fallacy for the same reason that any ad hominem is a fallacy. It pretends that someone's race automatically commits them to saying false things. More precisely, it pretends that being white automatically commits white people to saying false things.

THE MYTH OF BLACK WEAKNESS

Earlier I described how neoracists try to redefine "racism." To qualify as racism, they say, discrimination, stereotyping, prejudice, hatred, or hostility needs to target people who lack power in society. But, they say, only white people have power in society. As a result, neoracists insist that discriminating against white people on the basis of their skin color, promoting white stereotypes, being prejudiced against white people, and expressing hatred or hostility toward them on account of their race doesn't count as racism.

This neoracist line of reasoning displays a myth about power: I call this the Myth of Black Weakness.

How Neoracists Stereotype Black People

I've already talked about the way neoracists stereotype white people. But they also stereotype black people.

Neoracists depict black people as being emotionally fragile—almost like children. We saw one form of this stereotype in the Myth of Inherited Trauma, which claims that black people alive today are personally traumatized by the experience of slavery even though they themselves never experienced it. According to neoracists, black people live in a state of chronic victimhood—a permanent condition, almost like a genetic disease, that they can't bounce back from and that they lack the power to move past.

As a result, neoracists depict black people as being in a state of constant emotional vulnerability and need. Robin DiAngelo even says that white people should never cry around black people because it might traumatize them further by evoking the cultural memory of false rape accusations—accusations that white women advanced against black men behind veils of tears.

Similarly, some neoracists have suggested that black people aren't inclined toward hard work or self-reliance. The National Museum of African American History and Culture even included a graphic on its website (which was later removed) claiming that hard work, self-reliance, and the nuclear family were attributes of "white dominant culture." Museum officials claimed that the graphic was inspired by a chart in the 1978 book *White Awareness: Handbook for Anti-Racism Training* by Judith H. Katz.

A similar book, *Dismantling Racism: A Workbook for Social Change Groups* by Kenneth Jones and Tema Okun, was adopted by the former schools chancellor of New York City, Richard Carranza, as part of an administrator training program. The book lists several traits of "White Supremacy Culture," including perfectionism, objectivity, and "worship of the written word," which it describes as a tendency to more highly value people with strong documentation and writing skills.

It's difficult to imagine a more insulting and demeaning image of black people—or of any people. Yet this stereotype is a part of the neoracist worldview. It's part of their Myth of Black Weakness.

The Many Kinds of Power

Connected to this assumption is the view that black Americans lack power. I'm going to adopt a working definition of power for the purposes of this conversation: one's ability to enforce one's will on others. There are many different kinds of power. Different people, moreover, have different kinds of power in differing degrees. People even have different kinds and degrees of power in different situations. Power dynamics can change from one room to another or from one moment to the next.

When people think about power in a society, they tend to think about political power, understood roughly as the ability to shape public policy to one's benefit. Political power can be measured in terms of how much representation a group of people has in the government. But political power is only one kind of power. There's also economic power, understood roughly as the ability to use wealth to effect change.

In addition to political and economic power, there's also what I would call "cultural power": roughly, the ability to shape the norms and values of society in a way that benefits a particular group. Cultural power is impossible to measure and less tangible than political or economic power, but it is no less important. Much of our social status, as well as our opportunities in life, are mediated by intangible elements of culture rather than directly influenced by politics or by wealth.

One way of gauging a group's cultural power is by looking at their ability to enforce social norms that punish speech and behavior they find uniquely offensive. For instance, when American Christians were able to keep ideas that offended them from being broadcast on network television or radio, that was a manifestation of cultural power. The inability to measure this power made it no less real.

Who Has Power in America?

Let's return to the idea that different people have different kinds of power in differing degrees. Even though it's hard to make generalizations because power dynamics are so fluid, we might try to identify some general tendencies in American society.

Political Power: At the time of writing, the four most populous cities in America all have black mayors. Blacks have roughly proportional representation in the House of Representatives, somewhat higher-than-proportional representation on the Supreme Court, and lower-than-proportional representation in the Senate. Taking all of these data points together, the political power of blacks and whites is broadly comparable.

Economic Power: White Americans have far more economic power, measured in terms of wealth, than either black Americans or Hispanics.

Cultural Power: When it comes to cultural power, I would argue that black Americans as a group have more than white people—especially white conservatives and moderates. A few examples will illustrate the point.

Consider the fact that in the past two decades the practice of blackface—which a significant portion of the black community finds offensive—went from something routinely seen on television and in movies to something that virtually no one would consider doing for any reason. In the 2000s and early 2010s, Jimmy Fallon, Jimmy Kimmel, Fred Armisen, Ashton Kutcher, Robert Downey Jr., Sarah Silverman, and many other celebrities performed in blackface. As of 2023, my guess is that not a single one of them would dream of ever doing it again. That is an indication of the cultural power of the black American community.

Compare this with, for example, the lack of cultural power possessed by the Mormon community in America. *The Book of Mormon*, a Broadway musical about Mormon missionaries in Africa is the thirteenth-longest-running Broadway show in American history. The irreverent musical was written by the creators of *South Park*, Trey Parker and Matt Stone, who are not themselves Mormon. The show includes lots of humor at the expense of Mormon culture as well as beliefs they hold sacred. The Mormon community reacted surprisingly well to this musical, even taking out ads in the playbills. Still, some Mormons were privately offended. We should not confuse the Mormon community's surprisingly good-natured reaction to the show with the claim that they had any power to prevent it. A Broadway show that was analogously offensive to the black community could not get off the ground. As if to prove my point, it was ultimately *The Book of Mormon*'s portrayal of Africans—not its main target by a long shot—that led the showrunners to actually alter the script and rewrite the parts that offended some black observers.

Another example: In March 2022, various media outlets were busy trying to empathetically understand how comedian Chris Rock's infamous G.I. Jane joke about Jada Pinkett Smith at the Academy Awards could be offensive to black women. NBC News ran an op-ed titled "Hey Chris Rock, I'm a Bald Black Woman—and It's Not a Joke." *USA Today* ran a piece called "Jada Pinkett Smith, Chris Rock and Why His Hair Joke Was So Problematic." Meanwhile, the same week, comedian Jon Stewart ran a segment literally titled "The Problem with White People" on his

TV show. Yet none of those same media outlets seem interested in how such a title might be offensive to white people. Nor did Stewart have to worry about being socially punished—about, say, losing his reputation or job—however many white people he may have offended. Think likewise of wokewashing—the equation of blackness with goodness and whiteness with evil—in Hollywood, as well as the general acceptance of anti-white sentiment in elite American institutions. All of this indicates that white people who are offended by anti-white tropes (especially conservative and moderate whites) currently have little cultural power.

Whether you agree or disagree on every detail, the foregoing points illustrate that the question "Who has power in America?" merits a far more complex answer than simply "white people." To insist otherwise is to misunderstand the many kinds of power that exist in a society, and the complex ways those kinds of power are distributed among different groups.

So far I've argued that blacks and whites have similar levels of political power: whites have more economic power, and blacks have more cultural power. You might agree with these statements but still think that economic power matters more than cultural power. That's reasonable. But even if we accept that that's true, the claim that "white Americans" hold more economic power is misleading. The top 10 percent of American households own 68 percent of the nation's wealth, while the bottom 50 percent of households hold only 3 percent. If we are considering wealth to be a proxy for economic power, then we must contend with the fact that the majority of Americans of every race have basically no economic power whatsoever—no ability to throw around their wealth so as to impose their will on society.

Neoracists believe that white people have power and black people don't, and that this asymmetry in group power means that black people can't be truly racist and white people can't truly be victims of racism. The crux of the problem with this view is that we, as individuals, never experience having the average traits of our racial group. We experience only the lives that we have individually. If you're a working class white person, what good does it do you that other white people who you will never meet control vast amounts of wealth? How do you, as an individual, benefit from the fact that people like Bill Gates and Jeff Bezos belong to the same race as you? The truth is that you don't. Yet you suffer the loss of neoracist sympathy just the same. The "prejudice plus power" equation, they say, applies equally to you. From the neoracist view, tens of millions of white Americans share in the downsides of being viewed as powerful without sharing in the upsides of actually having power. That is a deep problem with neoracism as a philosophy, and it is a deep political problem for the country as a whole.

6

Solving the Problem
of Racism in America

We've now seen the narrative that neoracists endorse. And we've seen the many ways in which this narrative betrays both the principles and the goals of the civil rights movement. We've also covered the myths and fallacies that undergird this narrative.

There's a different narrative of race and racism in America— a story of missed opportunities to achieve a colorblind state. Key chapters in that story include the founding of our republic on the backs of slaves, the ratification of a weaker version of the Fourteenth Amendment that opened the door to Jim Crow, a Supreme Court decision that upheld the constitutionality of racial segregation (*Plessy*), another Supreme Court decision that fell short of affirming colorblindness (*Brown*), the betrayal of colorblindness at just the moment when the civil rights movement was enjoying its greatest success, and the rise of race consciousness that's turned elite American institutions into neoracist strongholds.

This series of missed opportunities describes what I view as the real problem of racism in America: our society keeps failing to enshrine colorblindness as its guiding ethos. It is this ongoing failure that has allowed state-sanctioned racism to emerge again and again in new and different forms—most recently throughout the movement I've been calling neoracism.

So if that's the real problem of racism in America—our society's failure to enshrine colorblindness—how do we solve it?

The short answer is that we need to seize the current opportunity to recommit ourselves to the principles of the civil rights movement. We need to condemn neoracism for what it is: racism in anti-racist clothing. We need to encourage employers, decision-makers, and educators to implement colorblind processes that eliminate the opportunity for racism against minorities. We need to support class-based policies instead of race-based policies. We need to embrace our common humanity and the colorblind philosophy that follows from it. We need to embody that philosophy in race-neutral public policies. And we need to strive to ensure that our personal relationships don't get infected with toxic race thinking of any sort.

RECONCEIVING DIVERSITY

If American society were to commit itself to colorblindness in our personal lives and in our public policy, would there be any room for proactively promoting racial diversity? In other words, is racial diversity a goal worth pursuing?

In the colorblind philosophy, racial diversity is neither inherently good nor inherently bad. We often hear slogans such as "diversity is our strength." As nice as these platitudes may sound, race is a meaningless trait that does not map neatly onto anything that we should care about. Therefore, racial diversity, by itself, is neutral. We may rehearse these nice-sounding platitudes, but nobody really believes that Earth, Wind & Fire would have been inherently better if they had added a white musician. Nor does anyone believe the Beatles were in desperate need of a Hispanic bandmate to round out their sound. Nor does anyone go to their favorite Mexican restaurant and think, "That would have been a fantastic meal except that their kitchen needs some white people."

Clearly, racial diversity isn't inherently good or bad. Its goodness or badness depends on what comes along with it in any given instance. It is good insofar as it helps us accomplish other worthy goals. For example, it's a good thing that the NYPD is racially diverse because effective policing depends in part on the perceived legitimacy of the police. A police force that consisted of all white men would not be perceived as legitimate by a population as racially diverse as New York City's. Does that mean the government should impose racial diversity in police forces by changing standards of entry? Ideally, no. We want police forces that maintain race-neutral standards of entry *and* are racially diverse. But insofar as there is an inherent trade-off between those two goals—and there very well could be in some cases—it could make sense to compromise on the former.

Compare policing to a job like firefighting. Here, the goal is simply to get the best people for the job. The fire doesn't care whether you're white, black, Hispanic, or Asian. Nor does the job depend on the public perception of legitimacy like policing does.

Here, the colorblind merit principle should reign supreme. I would argue that most jobs and spaces in society are more like firefighting than policing. We should generally want to get the best people for the job, and in most cases the ability to do the job does not depend on public perception.

STIGMATIZING RACIST TALK

How do we confront and combat neoracism in our daily thoughts, feelings, and actions? One way is to stigmatize expressions of racism—*any* type of racism. Right now in American society calling a black person the N-word is highly stigmatized. This is a very good thing. But racial slurs directed at white people aren't. This neoracist double standard is toxic.

People are understandably angered by racial double standards. Racial double standards, no matter how understandable their origins may be, perpetuate unfairness. If we want a more just society, and a society with less racial tension and racial resentment, then we need to treat all forms of racial stereotyping and insult as toxic. There are two ways of collapsing the double standard: we need to either (a) stigmatize racial slurs of all sorts equally or (b) destigmatize racial slurs of all sorts equally.

I don't want to see the double standard collapsed in the direction of destigmatization. I don't favor increasing the number of racial slurs directed against people in our society—any people, whatever their race. I favor a society in which directing racial slurs at people is stigmatized and in which people self-govern their speech in ways that decrease racist expressions directed at any groups.

I do nevertheless appreciate that some people might disagree and favor (b) over (a). In fact, I'm willing to concede that there are contexts in which people agree to destigmatize racist talk—comedy clubs, for instance. But these contexts are the exception that proves the rule. In general, we need to curb people's worst instincts for bigotry and righteous anger by creating strong social disincentives for indulging in them, and that means it's better for us to stigmatize racist talk across the board.

You might object: "Coleman, people of color are forced to think about their race all the time; they're reminded frequently that they're not white, and this constant reminder of their race is burdensome and harmful. White people have the luxury of ignoring their whiteness. Surely, justice demands that we remedy this unbalanced situation by strongly encouraging white people to reflect on their race as well."

While I'd agree with the general point that it is wise to reflect on the advantages and disadvantages one has been given in life, this specific objection fails to persuade me. In fact, this argument shoots itself in the foot. It concedes one of my central contentions: that constantly paying attention to race is burdensome and harmful. If this is true, then why would we want to increase the sum total of this burden in society at large? Think of it this way: Imagine that a certain percentage of people in our society were suffering from some harmful disease. Would we conclude that the remedy was to spread the disease to the entire population or to keep it contained and cure the people suffering from it?

What motivates the perverse logic of this objection isn't a concern for real justice. What motivates it instead is the law of retaliation disguised as a concern for real justice—revenge masquerading as empathy. It's a mindset that supposes the way to remedy a harm is only by imposing an equal and opposite harm: if I strike you, you strike me; if I steal from you, you steal from me; if I kill your child, you kill mine. By this line of reasoning, the only way to remedy one kind of injustice is by replacing it with another.

But cycles of ethnic violence around the world show us again and again that a society doesn't overcome injustice by creating new forms of it. They show us again and again how simplistic and outmoded this way of thinking is—a way of thinking that leads to interminable hatred generation after generation. This perverse conception of justice is what's at the heart of neoracist ideology—the perverse logic of taking an eye for an eye.

FIGHTING RACIAL DISCRIMINATION AGAINST MINORITIES

When I was in college, I had a great philosophy professor with whom I took multiple classes. Whenever we turned in essays, she used a blind grading system to guarantee that she did not know whose essay she was grading. After she assigned a grade, only then could she see whose paper it was. This way, she eliminated the possibility of gender bias, racial bias, and even bias against particular students for any idiosyncratic reason.

Given what we know about discrimination against minorities in society as a whole, it is astounding to me that blinding processes like this are not universal. We saw in chapter five that minorities face a large amount of discrimination in the labor market. Such discrimination also exists in higher education. A group of researchers sent over 6,500 emails to over 4,000 professors at the top 259 colleges in America. These emails, requesting to meet the professor for mentorship, were identical except for racially- and gender-coded names.

Minorities were less likely to receive a response in every field of study except for fine arts, where white men were at a disadvantage. Overall, Chinese women and Indians experienced the most severe discrimination. Interestingly, aside from Chinese professors, all other minority professors discriminated against minority students just as much as white professors did—suggesting that more faculty diversity does not equal less discrimination against minority students.

In the past several years, corporations, nonprofits, and schools have devoted enormous amounts of time and money to "combating racism" by creating diversity and inclusion task forces—despite little evidence that such efforts actually reduce discrimination against minorities. Almost no effort or money has been put toward creating blinded grading systems such as the one my philosophy professor used—despite the fact that we have compelling evidence that racial discrimination is rampant in these kinds of processes.

My message for anyone who is a key decision-maker at an institution: If you care about fighting racism, create blind processes wherever possible. Help yourself be objective by blinding yourself to data that might bias you. Granted, this approach is more practical in some domains than others and is simply impossible in many parts of life. But there is an enormous amount of low-hanging fruit here that has not been picked. There is no reason, for instance, why high school and college professors cannot implement blind grading systems whenever possible. Employers who care about fighting racism can enact systems to blind themselves to the names on the résumés of prospective job applicants.

This may be hard or costly to implement. But if the level of concern about racism expressed by elite institutions in 2020 was in any way genuine, then key decision-makers should acknowledge the importance of colorblind processes and should be willing to think creatively in order to implement them.

THE LIMITS OF EQUITY

Neoracists want a society in which the racial representation in any given sector matches the racial representation in the general population. Here, for instance, is Ibram X. Kendi:

> If Black people make up 13.2 percent of the US population, then Black people should make up somewhere close to 13 percent of the Americans killed by the police, somewhere close to 13 percent of the Americans sitting in prisons, somewhere close to owning 13 percent of US wealth.

> If we could wave a magic wand and create such a society—without racially discriminating, without creating a monocul-

ture, without violating anyone's rights, and without causing any additional suffering—then we would be crazy not to. Such a society would have less racial resentment and racial profiling, and more racial harmony. But there are no magic wands in the real world. And in the real world, the means by which we try to achieve equality of outcome are as important as the end itself.

There are two problems with efforts to achieve equity in the real world. First, in order to achieve equal outcomes across the board, you would have to kill cultural diversity. As we saw in chapter five, cultural differences between groups create benign disparities—that is, disparities not caused by racism. That will continue to be true as long as we live in a multicultural society (as opposed to a monoculture). We cannot celebrate cultural diversity while also expecting people of different cultural backgrounds to perform identically across the board.

Second, achieving equity simply by fiat—that is, by lowering standards of entry for underrepresented groups—does nothing to equip people with the knowledge, skills, and habits required to succeed. Equity by fiat is merely the illusion of equity. Quotas can be easily achieved by racially rigging a process—that is, by lowering the bar of entry for certain races and raising the bar for others. But that does little to address the underlying causes of racial disparity.

If as a society we are going to strive for equity, then we must keep two things at the front of our minds. First, we need to understand that there is an inherent limit to how close we can get to equal outcomes in a multicultural society, and that's OK. Benign disparities will abound, and we should pay more attention to the fairness of processes than to the equality of results.

Second, the way that we progress toward equity matters as much as the goal itself. We need to recommit ourselves to the principle of race-neutral merit and work toward a society in which more and more disadvantaged people are able to clear meritocratic benchmarks as a result of actually possessing the skills required to compete in the economy. Anything less is an illusion. (That said, I very much support affirmative action in the original sense of the term: aggressively recruiting minority candidates and candidates from less-privileged backgrounds and then judging them by race-neutral standards.)

The majority of effort channeled toward achieving racial equity hasn't been applied to the part of life that has the biggest influence on people's skills and mindsets: namely birth to eighteen years of age. Think, for instance, of affirmative action. It typically kicks in when young adults are applying to college. By that point in life, many skills, attitudes, and habits have already been formed. We can have a much bigger impact on people at younger ages.

Efforts to achieve true equity should focus instead on high-quality kindergarten and pre-K, high-quality weekend learning programs, high-quality charter schools, and high-quality after-school tutoring. By "high-quality" I mean programs, schools, and tutoring that focus on skills development.

If we want to move toward true equity, we need to intervene early and provide programs that close the skills gap. If we do that—if we equip people in society with the skills they need to flourish—then, within limits, a shrinkage of outcome gaps will follow naturally.

The Uncomfortable Truth about Affirmative Action

When reality makes us queasy, we use euphemisms. During the George W. Bush administration, for instance, people began using the term "enhanced interrogation" to refer to torture. Why? Because unlike the word "torture," the phrase "enhanced interrogation" could mean anything. It doesn't call to mind bloodcurdling screams and hellish torture chambers. The phrase therefore provided cover for the abuses that it referred to.

We use the phrase "affirmative action" for the same reason. It's a euphemism. It's a phrase that could mean literally anything. If you didn't know what it meant, the words themselves would give you no hint. The truth is that we don't really want to call to mind what the actual policy is, namely racial discrimination. We don't want to see how the sausage is made. And the bureaucratic phrase affirmative action provides rhetorical cover for the practice of discriminating against people on the basis of their race—practices like the one described by a personnel secretary at a defense contractor:

> When receiving an application, I was instructed to thank the person, wait until they left, then pencil in their race in the upper right-hand corner. You see, we had "enough" whites and Hispanics at the facility; we needed more blacks. If the applicant was not black, no matter what his qualifications, the application went into an inactive file to be considered no further.

You can get as granular as you'd like about the conditions for affirmative action—when it is or isn't permitted, how it can or can't be practiced, or to what degree it can or can't be implemented—but you can't get around the fact that affirmative action always involves people making decisions like the one above in back rooms and hushed tones.

The euphemism affirmative action has enabled this form of racial discrimination to gain public support. To get a sense for how effective the euphemism has been, consider the results of two surveys about college admissions: one published by the Pew Research Center, the other by Gallup. Both surveys were published in February 2019. Both surveys asked more than 6,500 respondents across the United States how they felt about universities using race as a factor in college admissions.

Pew asked 6,637 American adults: "Do you think race/ethnicity should be a major factor, minor factor, or not a factor in college admissions?"

Gallup asked 6,502 American adults: "Do you generally favor or oppose affirmative action programs for racial minorities?"

In the Pew survey, 73 percent of respondents said race/ethnicity should not be a factor in college admissions. But 61 percent of respondents to the Gallup survey said they supported affirmative action programs for racial minorities.

According to one poll, then, most Americans favor a color-blind admissions process, yet according to another poll conducted simultaneously, most Americans favor a race-conscious admissions process. You can't have it both ways. Could there have been a sampling error? That seems unlikely for organizations as careful as Gallup and Pew. The more likely explanation is that most

Americans find the label "affirmative action" more appealing than a frank description of what affirmative action is—a description like "making race a factor in admissions." I'm sure more Americans supported "enhanced interrogation" than "torture" as well.

The euphemism has made a difference in public perception about what the practice really is. That's understandable. When we look at the policy for what it really is, we *should* feel discomfort. We should approach affirmative action the same way we approach enhanced interrogation: look past the label and examine the reality.

At the time of writing, racial preferences are alive and well. That said, they are slated for a major Supreme Court decision soon in the case *Students for Fair Admissions Inc. v. University of North Carolina, et al.* The case petition gives an inside look into the admissions process at the university:

> In reviewing applications, admissions officers focus intently (and sometimes crudely) on an applicant's race, as revealed by online chats among admissions officers.
>
> "I just opened a brown girl who's an 810 [SAT]."
>
> "If its brown and above a 1300 [SAT] put them in for [the] merit/Excel [scholarship]."
>
> "Still yes, give these brown babies a shot at these merit $$."
>
> "I am reading an Am. Ind."
>
> "[W]ith these [URM] kids, I'm trying to at least give them the chance to compete even if the [extracurriculars] and essays are just average."
>
> "I don't think I can admit or defer this brown girl."
>
> "perfect 2400 SAT All 5 on AP one B in 11th"

"Brown?!"

"Heck no. Asian."

"Of course. Still impressive."

"I just read a blk girl who is an MC and Park nominee."

How many people support affirmative action simply because they don't know what goes on in admissions offices? Princeton sociologist Thomas Espenshade studied a representative sample of elite colleges and found that when other factors were held equal, Asians and whites had to score 450 and 310 SAT points higher than black applicants, respectively, to have the same odds of being admitted.

Imagine if every college rejection letter included the honest reasons for rejection: "If you had been black rather than Asian, we would have accepted you." How long would the policy survive? Probably not long. In some sense, it is only secrecy that keeps the policy alive. Yet if a combination of secrecy and euphemism is what keeps the policy alive, then it is hard to argue that the policy has real public support. People's attitudes change about something when they can witness its real effects and adequately measure its costs. Racial preferences maintain public support only because they happen behind closed doors and under the cover of a convenient euphemism. It's a policy that most people of goodwill wouldn't support if they knew what it actually involves.

You might object, "Coleman, you misunderstand the nature of affirmative action. It was never intended to be a permanent policy. It was merely supposed to be a temporary corrective for the effects of past discrimination."

The original vision for affirmative action was for it to serve as training wheels on the path to a colorblind society. This idea was echoed by Justice Sandra Day O'Connor in the 2003 Supreme Court case *Grutter v. Bollinger*: "We expect that 25 years from now, the use of racial preferences will no longer be necessary to further the interest [in student body diversity] approved today." But in practical terms, it's very difficult to enact this commitment to impermanence. When a policy like affirmative action has been ensconced in society for decades, removing it is difficult. Its supporters stop seeing it merely as a means to an end and begin seeing it as an end in itself. So it has been with race-conscious policies like affirmative action.

Yet affirmative action has done little to help the truly disadvantaged. Fifty years into affirmative action, the percentage of students from low-income backgrounds attending Ivy League schools remains in the low single digits. One study showed that between 2000 and 2011, less than 5 percent of Harvard's student population came from the bottom quintile of income, while about 70 percent of their students came from the top quintile. Yet 14 percent of Harvard students are black—about the same as the percentage in the general population. The great majority of black students attending a university like Harvard are not coming from anything one could call a disadvantage. Indeed, a disproportionately high percentage of Harvard students are not even descended from American slaves but from post-1965 African or Caribbean immigrants.

Princeton sociologist Thomas Espenshade estimates that in any given year, only about 1 percent of the nation's black and Hispanic eighteen-year-olds benefit from affirmative action in college admissions. The other 99 percent either don't graduate from high school, don't go to college, or don't go to colleges selective enough to "need" racial preferences. To make matters worse, the 1 percent of black and Hispanic students who are admitted to highly selective colleges often don't perform as well as their peers:

> Students who are admitted through affirmative action (and who often have weaker academic credentials than their peers) are more likely to graduate toward the bottom of their class. Analyzing data from eight elite colleges (five private, three public) from 1999 and 2003, my colleague Alexandria Walton Radford and I found that one-half of black students and one-third of Hispanic students graduated in the bottom 20 percent of their class.

How is it that policies like affirmative action have done so little to help the truly disadvantaged? My hypothesis is that the people whom race-based policies help most are people who don't need the extra help—people who are already well-off. In whatever way those policies are skewed—whether to benefit whites or non-whites—the people who gain the most from race-based policies are the ones who are already well positioned to reap society's benefits—not the truly disadvantaged.

What affirmative action does accomplish is to provide elite institutions like Harvard with a pretense of social concern. They get to say that 14 percent of their students are black. This in turn enables them to portray themselves as champions against inequality even though they do little to invite and integrate students who are truly disadvantaged.

On the whole, it's not clear that lowering the bar of entry for students of color even benefits them. At some level, going to a more prestigious school seems like an obvious benefit. You get access to a better network of people and resources from which to build a career.

But there are hidden costs to lowering the bar for any particular student or group of students. A major cost is that you virtually guarantee that that student will be at the *bottom* of their entering class in terms of academic preparedness, general knowledge, and skills. You virtually guarantee that such students will be treading water among skilled swimmers.

If it's true that admitting a group of students under lower standards puts them at the bottom of their class, then that should be measurable. Either they should get lower grades than other students, graduate at a lower rate, or show some other sign of academic weakness relative to their peers.

In 2012, a group of social scientists at Duke University studied this topic and found an interesting and disheartening result. They found that black students entering Duke initially got worse grades than their white peers in the first year—exactly what you'd expect if you believe that admission standards predict performance. But by the end of four years, they found that black students had substantially closed the GPA gap with their white peers. An affirmative action success story, right?

Wrong. It turns out that the reason black students as a whole performed better as college progressed was because so many of them switched from harder majors to easier majors. Incoming freshmen of all races showed similar levels of interest in hard sciences. But the attrition rate out of difficult majors for black students was far larger than for white students. Over 54 percent of black men who initially planned to major in hard sciences eventually switched to the humanities or social sciences. The figure for white men was less than 8 percent. (Women showed the same disparity but to a lesser degree.)

How do we know the attrition from the more difficult majors was a product of lower standards of entry, rather than some other race-specific cause (like racism)? Well, if the problem is lower standards of entry, then it should apply to *any* identifiable group of students who are admitted under lower standards—including, for example, legacy admits (that is, people admitted because their parents or siblings also attended). Sure enough, the Duke researchers found the same effect for this group: an illusory convergence of GPA with their non-legacy peers resulting from a higher attrition rate out of hard majors to easier majors.

Whatever benefits racial preferences in college admissions have passed on to black and Hispanic students, it has certainly hurt many of them as well. No doubt, many students who would have followed through on their hard science majors at a less prestigious school ended up majoring in humanities simply in order to survive—hardly the intended result.

Affirmative action has been a quick fix that masks the underlying issue. There is no end run around meritocracy that will yield the desirable equity that affirmative action aims to achieve. To help people succeed you have to help them acquire the skills needed to be successful. That is a difficult but worthy task. But you cannot declare victory simply by lowering the bar by which success at that task is measured.

The Limits of Race-Based Policies

In the wake of George Floyd's murder in 2020, governments and corporations wanted to signal that they were sensitive and responsive to the problem of racism, so they began instituting race-based programs. Companies began announcing that they were going to start investing more in diversity, and there was a call for corporations to add more people of color to their boards. The state of California announced that it was going to require the boards of publicly traded companies headquartered in the state to be racially diverse. Microsoft announced that it was going to double the number of black employees in managerial positions, and CBS announced that it was establishing a racial diversity quota for its writers' rooms.

Race-based policies (as opposed to class-based policies) tend to benefit the people of that race who need them the least. Think of who benefited from the race-based policies implemented in response to George Floyd's murder. Overwhelmingly, they were relatively wealthy individuals who had little in common with Floyd—not income, not background, not position in society, not job description. The thing they had in common with George Floyd was skin color, and many of them—Hispanics, Asians, and white women—did not even share that.

A poor man from a poor neighborhood was brutally killed by the police, and in response a group of relatively wealthy people, who would likely cross the street if they saw George Floyd coming their way at night, positioned themselves to become even more wealthy by joining the boards of publicly traded companies. And this wasn't called avarice or opportunism, but *justice*—a noble act and a legitimate way of redressing what had been done to Floyd.

The gains from race-based policies adopted in response to the George Floyd murder were overwhelmingly captured by elites of color—high-income, highly educated people of color who were already well positioned to reap society's benefits—while poor communities had their police forces dismantled and defunded. My hypothesis is that what's true of the race-based policies instituted in response to Floyd's murder is true of race-based policies in general. Whether those policies are skewed to benefit whites or non-whites, the people they end up benefiting most are, by and large, those already standing close to the tap out of which societal benefits flow.

Anti-Racist Alternatives to Affirmative Action

Affirmative action hasn't succeeded in closing the skills gap. At best, it delivers only the illusion of equality without the substance. The reason is that it doesn't focus on building habits, attitudes, and skills at crucial developmental ages. Too much of the money and effort that's been channeled toward securing greater racial equity over the past several decades hasn't been applied to that part of life during which we can have the biggest impact: birth to eighteen years of age. Affirmative action effectively kicks in only after most of a person's skills, habits, and attitudes have been formed.

We need an educational system that helps develop those habits and attitudes early in children's lives. As I've noted, we should be channeling our resources to programs that focus on skill development during the critical formative years: high-quality pre-K and kindergarten programs, high-quality weekend learning programs, high-quality charter schools, and high-quality after-school tutoring programs.

Princeton sociologist Thomas Espenshade, coauthor of *No Longer Separate, Not Yet Equal*, has a similar idea:

> If affirmative action is abolished, selective colleges and universities will face a stark choice. They can try to manufacture diversity by giving more weight in admissions to those factors that are sometimes close substitutes for race—for example, having overcome disadvantage in a poor urban neighborhood. Or they can take a far bolder step: putting their endowments and influence behind a comprehensive effort to close the learning gap that starts at birth. Higher education has a responsibility for all of education.

What Espenshade describes is a way that elite colleges and universities can help secure true equity: they can use their resources to support an educational system that helps children and young adults master the skills they need to excel.

But how do we actually do this, practically? The Harvard economist Roland Fryer has done some of the most groundbreaking but neglected work on this question. After studying thirty-nine charter schools in New York City, Fryer identified five variables that correlated with success: (1) frequent teacher feedback, (2) the use of data to guide instruction, (3) high-dosage tutoring, (4) increased school time, and (5) a culture of high expectations.

Observational data such as this is interesting, but has a fatal flaw that I explain in detail in Appendix D: you can never control for all the preexisting differences between the kids who end up at the better charter schools and the kids who end up at the worse ones—even with charter lotteries (which are not quite as random as they seem).

So Fryer went further. He gained unprecedented access to the Houston public school system and designed a randomized experiment. He took a set of sixteen low-performing schools—containing just over five thousand students—and created "matched pairs" of schools based on the relevant student demographics. He then randomly assigned one school in each pair to the control group and one to the treatment group.

Schools in the treatment group received complete overhauls based on the five principles learned from high-performing NYC charter schools: The principals were fired and replaced along with about half of the teachers. School days were lengthened. Extra tutoring was provided. Extra tests were given and the results were used to tailor each student's tutoring. And a culture of excellence and high expectations was consciously fostered from the top down. The overall result was a 0.103 standard deviation increase in math scores for black students, with even larger gains for elementary-aged students, and students from lower socioeconomic backgrounds.

More research along these lines is needed, but the lessons so far appear to be threefold: First, early intervention should become the mantra for those of us who want to close the skills gap.

Second, charter schools—a favorite target of teacher's unions and the progressive wing of the Democratic Party—are not the enemy of public schools, much less the enemy of disadvantaged kids. And third, fostering a culture of high expectations is a crucial component of closing the skills gap. The "tough love," high-discipline approach—unpopular as it may be in elite academic and policy-making circles—is the way to go.

Lowering standards for people of color translates into a benefit for them and for society as a whole only if the entire system is rigged to sustain the illusion that we've closed the skills gap: from K–12 education, to college, to employment, and standards of professional evaluation. But you always have to confront the constraints of reality somewhere. If you have an educational system with lower standards for some groups, then those groups end up being ill prepared to confront the unforgiving demands of the real world. A disease like cancer isn't fooled by a pretense of competence. Neither is a professional sports team whose roster is put together based purely on merit. If you don't have the relevant skills in these domains, then you and the people around you suffer.

There are many domains in which people aren't willing to harbor doubts about the people they're working with. If someone wants a competent doctor or lawyer, a system like affirmative action incentivizes them to opt for a non-minority individual. Why? Because affirmative action raises questions in people's minds about the competence of minorities. If people know that the standards are lower for minorities, they can't feel confident that a minority doctor or lawyer really is the best person for the job. Policies like affirmative action incentivize people to look at a black doctor or lawyer and think about his race as opposed to his competence. That's hardly a benefit to people of color.

What's better than affirmative action—what would truly benefit people of color—is an educational system that helps children develop the habits, attitudes, and skills they need to flourish in adult life. This is an educational system that's consistent with the principles and goals of the civil rights movement—an educational system aimed at progressing toward true equity, not the false-outcome equity favored by neoracists.

TWO ROADS: ANTI-RACISM VS NEORACISM

When I look at the current racial landscape of American society, I feel sick at heart. I dread the possibility of black identity becoming tied to a rehearsed sense of victimhood, and of people of color never allowing themselves to participate fully in the privileges of freedom. I worry that we'll never accept that we've won the battle for civil rights; that we'll become so wedded to the idea that we're victims that we'll render ourselves incapable of embarking on the project of flourishing—that we'll be so limited in our conception of who we are that we'll prevent ourselves from enjoying the fruits of victory.

The goal of fighting a war is to eventually be in a position to enjoy the fruits of peace. That's what makes all the hardship and sacrifice worthwhile: to be able to return home from the battlefield and get on with the business of living, loving, and flourishing. The vision of people winning a war—and not any war, but a just war—yet being incapable of accepting that they've emerged victorious fills me with sadness.

Neoracists don't want racial peace, but endless ideological war. When we see neoracism for what it is—racism in anti-racist clothing—we see why neoracists fail to support colorblind policies that would actually eliminate racism, and why they reject the colorblind principles that motivated the civil rights movement.

Racial strife is what fuels the neoracist industry. Neoracists need people to believe in monstrous and ongoing racial oppression. If racism were eliminated from society, neoracists would be out of a job: they'd no longer have anyone or anything to accuse; their agenda would lose social relevance, and they'd no longer be able to garner the cultural power they crave.

It's only by perpetuating interracial hatred—by continuing to make old racial wounds seem fresh, by spreading the myth that our society has made little progress toward eliminating racism against people of color, and by exaggerating the threat of white supremacy—that neoracists can continue getting what they want. It's only by doing these things that neoracists can continue feeling justified in inflicting pain and suffering on the targets of their bigotry so that they can continue depicting themselves as heroes.

At this moment in American history, we have a choice. We can follow neoracists down the path of endless racial strife, or we can recommit ourselves to the principles that motivated the civil rights movement—and not just the civil rights movement, but also the abolitionist movement and other movements around the world that oppose unjust discrimination. Those principles include a belief in our common humanity—the idea that what it takes for human beings to flourish has nothing essential to do with our skin color or ancestry or any of the other traits that people have used throughout history to divide themselves. And those principles include colorblindness—the idea that we should treat people without regard to race, both in our public policy and in our private lives.

Neoracists imagine that if we enact discriminatory policies for long enough we will finally balance the scales of history. We will be able to undo the past, give back to blacks what was taken from them for hundreds of years, and reach a state of racial "equity." But this is a dangerous fantasy.

Our nation's history shows us what will happen if we follow neoracists: we'll get an ethnically white core of the country that is every bit as angry and aggrieved about neoracist policies like the Restaurant Revitalization Fund and section 1005 of the American Rescue Plan as black Americans were about segregation and redlining. And just as the black American grievances were true and real, so will the white grievances be.

The neoracist road leads to a grim world in which whites and minorities eternally swap the roles of the oppressor and the oppressed, the guilty and the blameless—a world with no conception of the common good but one where individuals put the interests of their own racial group first, whatever the costs to others. The neoracist pursuit of false equity results in a war of all against all. Instead of realizing the dream of true racial equality, we'll realize a nightmare of endless racial strife.

The alternative is the dream I described earlier: a nation where people live in safety and enjoy the freedom to pursue their own happiness; a nation without second-class citizens, where the spirit of democracy prevails and politicians are held accountable to the people they serve; a nation that provides every child with a challenging education that develops the skills they need to grow into responsible adults; a nation where economic growth is steady, recessions are rare, and jobs are plentiful; a nation that provides quality health care to all its citizens and that invests heavily in caring for those who can't care for themselves; a nation where people are free to move from place to place and can afford to buy or rent homes in areas they want to live; a nation where people can enjoy their neighborhood without fear of crime and violence; a nation that leads the world in technological innovation but ensures that technology serves people, and not vice versa; a nation where people have many different beliefs but maintain a shared commitment to resolve disagreements with speech, not violence, and where people are free to engage in honest, open discussion without fear of being ostracized or canceled; a nation whose wise management of difficult trade-offs on issues like immigration, national security, and wealth inequality sets an example for the rest of the world; a nation in which children hear their grandparents' stories about the "old days" and marvel at the progress we've made.

ACKNOWLEDGMENTS

No book is a solo effort, and I've had plenty of help along the way. I'd like to thank Duane and Sabina, Drisana and Danielle, and Amsal for their steadfast support. Thank you Dr. William Jaworski and Ellen Fishbein at the Writing Coach team for their help with the writing process. I'd like to thank my editor, Helen Healey, as well as my literary agent, William Callahan, without whom this book could not have happened. And finally, thank you to the many friends and colleagues I have had the pleasure of engaging with over the past several years, some of whom looked at early drafts of the book: John McWhorter, Glenn Loury, Sam Harris, Steven Pinker, Thomas Chatterton Williams, Kmele Foster, Yascha Mounk, Noam Dworman, Tyler Cowen, Chloé Valdary, Ian Rowe, Jonathan Haidt, Tim Urban, Niall Ferguson, Wilfred Reilly, Scott Kaufman, Christian Gonzalez, Sam Koppelman, Amy Chua, Douglas Murray, Ayishat Akanbi, Rafael Mangual, and Jamil Jivani. Any remaining mistakes are my own.

APPENDIX A

Population genetics is among the most controversial areas of scientific inquiry. To be curious about the average genetic differences between populations of humans risks accusations of racism and race science. This is an understandable result of a recent history of race science run amok. In living memory, countries have used race science to support legally enforced separation of races, bans on intermarriage and sex, forced sterilization, and other heinous policies. No one of goodwill wants to repeat those injustices.

At the same time, there is nothing wrong with being curious about population genetics, and there is nothing wrong with applying the tools of scientific inquiry to the question of genetic differences. When it was discovered that some descendants of Europeans have Neanderthal DNA, or that some populations are more likely to be lactose intolerant than others, these reports went viral. Their virality is a testament to how common, and indeed normal, it is to be fascinated by this topic.

In chapter one, I made the following claim:

> Although each of us is genetically unique (barring identical twins), each of us also belongs to clusters of similar genomes whose similarity stems from the major out-of-Africa migrations that occurred tens of thousands of years ago. These clusters are not sharply separated from one another. They overlap a great deal, and therefore the boundaries between them are blurry. Using standard statistical tools, the strength of these genome clusters can be measured.

Here I want to expand in detail on exactly what I mean, for those who are curious.

With any data set, you can ask the questions: (1) Does the data form clusters? (2) How many clusters should the data be divided into? (3) How strong are the clusters? These are not open-ended questions on which everyone can have a valid subjective opinion. These are mathematical questions with mathematical answers.

Let's look at a simple example.

Scenario A: Imagine a room full of people. Your task is to measure their height (inches) and weight (pounds), and plot the data on an x-y coordinate graph. But here's the twist: the only people in the room are NFL linebackers and preschool children. Your graph will contain two visible clusters that do not overlap at all.

Scenario B: Now imagine performing the same experiment, but this time the room is filled with one thousand college freshmen. Your graph will not contain any noticeable clusters. You will simply find a mess of data from the shortest and lightest at one end, to the tallest and heaviest on the other.

Scenario C: Now imagine performing the test again. This time, the room is filled with three groups: seventeen-year-olds, fifteen-year-olds, and thirteen-years-olds. When you plot the data, you faintly perceive that there are three natural clusters, but you don't know where you would draw the line between them. The borders are messy rather than sharp. There is significant overlap.

In each scenario, it is possible to ask the three aforementioned questions: Does the data form clusters? How many clusters should the data be divided into? How strong are the clusters? The answer to the final question can come in the form of a clusteredness score. This score is a number between 0 and 1 (though it can also be measured from -1 to 1) that represents the strength of the clusters in the data.

In scenario A, the clusteredness score would be a 1. These clusters have sharp boundaries and no overlap. In scenario B, the clusteredness score would be 0 or very close to 0 (say, 0.01). Here, there are no clusters at all—no way to separate the data into chunks. Scenario C lies somewhere in between. It could have a clusteredness score from anywhere between 0.1 and 0.9. The lower the score, the weaker the clusters; the higher the score, the stronger the clusters. Whatever the score, these lines drawn are still not crisp distinctions. There is overlap between the clusters.

When the human genome was completely sequenced in 2003, it became theoretically possible to apply a cluster analysis to all of humanity (or to a representative sample). Instead of dealing with two variables (like height and weight), this analysis would deal with locations in the human genome that vary from individual to individual—hundreds or even thousands of locations where you might have one allele of a gene or another. Because this cluster analysis has so many variables, the math is more complicated in practice. But in principle it is no different from the simple scenarios described above. Either the genomes of the human beings separate into discrete categories (a score of 1); or there is no clustering to be found at all (a score of 0); or there is some clustering with significant overlap (a score between 0 and 1).

The first paper to do this came out in 2005: "Clines, Clusters, and the Effect of Study Design on the Inference of Human Population Structure." What researchers found is that the genomes of human beings do indeed form clusters. And the clusters they form broadly match our lay concept of race. They found anywhere between five, six, or seven clusters that correspond with the largest out-of-Africa migrations tens of thousands of years ago. When they measured the strength of these clusters using a few different methods, they got numbers ranging from about 0.6 to 0.8.

This puts humanity firmly in scenario C. Whether we want to call these clusters "races" or not is an issue of semantics. What is true is that we can each be placed in a cluster of genetically similar people, but those clusters bleed into one another significantly. This means that at least hundreds of millions of us are more genetically similar to the members of *another* cluster than we are to the members of "our own" cluster.

It is important to remember that lines between these clusters do not exist in the genomic data or in real life. The lines between clusters are abstract mathematical entities that can be drawn *no matter how weak the clustering is.* (They are similar to a line of best fit in this way. A line of best fit can be drawn over basically any assembly of data, no matter how scattered or random. You must go further and ask the question: How well does this line capture the trend of the data?) And even though the lines that separate one cluster from another don't exist in the real world, the fact that humans *can* be clustered with medium-high clustering strength represents an observation about the real world: namely, that the major out-of-Africa migrations—the separation of large populations for thousands of years—have left a real legacy in our genes.

The hard-core race realists of history have assumed that we are in scenario A—that there are hard-and-fast distinctions between the races. We are not. The hard-core social constructionists assume that we are in scenario B—that any way of clustering ourselves is as arbitrary as any another. That's also not the case. The truth is that we are in scenario C: there are valid ways of clustering ourselves that broadly match the major out-of-Africa migrations and the lay concept of race, but those clusters overlap and bleed into one another to such an extent that it is not possible to draw an actual line between races that has any meaning in the real world. In other words, no real-life racial sorting mechanism could be justified on even purely scientific grounds (to say nothing of political or moral grounds).

As a point of comparison, consider biological sex. Depending on how it's defined, anywhere from 98.3 percent to 99.9 of human beings are born unambiguously male or female, by which I mean that their chromosomal sex, XX or XY, aligns with their phenotypic sex, ovaries or testes. The rest are intersex or have one of a variety of rare conditions. If you were to take everyone's chromosomes, gonad type, etc.—and perform a clustering analysis on this data, it would yield two large clusters with an extremely high clusteredness score, barely distinguishable from a perfect 1. It is precisely because of this near-perfect clustering that we are able to sort males and females in real life.

That near-perfect clustering, along with the sharp boundary lines that result from it, is precisely what is absent in the case of population genetics and race.

APPENDIX B

———

A source of confusion that I will avoid in this book is the misleading word "post-racial." The "post" in post-racial suggests that there are two separate eras—a "racial" era, characterized by the presence of racism, and a "post-racial" era, characterized by its absence—and the important question is which era we are currently living in. Because colorblindness, in this framework, would make sense only during the second, racism-free era, many critics have dismissed colorblindness on the grounds that "we are not there yet"—that is, we have not yet eliminated racial prejudice.

About that much they are right—racism still exists. And racism against minorities in particular still exists. But they have framed the issue upside down. Colorblindness is not a synonym for the absence of racism. It is an ideology created in order to *fight* racism. As I show in chapter two, writers, activists, and politicians wielded the colorblind principle to great effect in the days of slavery and Jim Crow—eras that contained far more racism than exists today. The validity of the colorblind principle does not depend on how much racism exists or upon what era we are living in. Rather, it stands or falls based upon its soundness of the principle alone.

APPENDIX C

1. Give me the doll that you like to play with—(a) like best.

2. Give me the doll that is a nice doll.

3. Give me the doll that looks bad.

4. Give me the doll that is a nice color.

5. Give me the doll that looks like a white child.

6. Give me the doll that looks like a colored child.

7. Give me the doll that looks like a Negro child.

8. Give me the doll that looks like you.

According to the usual story, the results of this study showed that segregation lowered black kids' self-esteem, and Kenneth Clark's expert testimony in *Brown v. Board of Education* helped persuade the court of this fact.

In the course of researching this book, however, I read the study in its entirety and was surprised to find that it did *not* conclude that segregation harmed black kids' self-esteem. Quite the opposite, in fact. The kids who attended segregated southern schools had *higher* self-esteem than the northern kids who went to integrated schools. On every question relating to which doll is better, segregated black kids fared better than integrated black kids—by large amounts on requests 2 and 3, and by small amounts on requests 1 and 4.

TABLE 1		
Choices of Subjects in Northern (Mixed Schools) and Southern (Segregated Schools) Groups (Requests 1 Through 4)*		
CHOICE	NORTH, PERCENT	SOUTH, PERCENT
Request 1 (play with)		
Colored doll	28	37
White doll	72	62
Request 2 (nice doll)		
Colored doll	30	46
White doll	68	52
Request 3 (looks bad)		
Colored doll	71	49
White doll	17	16
Request 4 (nice color)		
Colored doll	37	40
White doll	63	57

*Individuals failing to make either choice not included, hence some percentages add up to less than 100.

At first, I assumed I had interpreted the data incorrectly. But it turns out that Kenneth and Mamie Clark agree with my reading of the data in the study. Here is their analysis of their data:

North-South Differences. From Table 1 it is clear that the southern children in segregated schools are less pronounced in their preference for the white doll, compared to the northern children's definite preference for this doll. Although still in a minority, a higher percentage of southern children, compared to northern, prefer to play with the colored doll or think that it is a "nice" doll. The critical ratio of this difference is not significant for request 1 but approaches significance for request 2.

They continue:

A significantly higher percentage (71) of the northern children, compared to southern children (49) think that the brown doll looks bad (critical ratio 3.68). Also a slightly higher percent of the southern children think that the brown doll has a "nice color," while more northern children think that the white doll has a "nice color."

In general, it may be stated that northern and southern children in these age groups tend to be similar in the degree of their preference for the white doll—with the northern children tending to be somewhat more favorable to the white doll than are the southern children. The southern children, however, in spite of their equal favorableness toward the white doll, are significantly less likely to reject the brown

doll (evaluate it negatively), as compared to the strong tendency for the majority of the northern children to do so. That
this difference is not primarily due to the larger number of
light children found in the northern sample is indicated by
more intensive analysis presented in the complete report.

If the independent variable in this study was whether the kids
attended segregated or integrated schools, and the dependent
variable was their self-esteem as judged by their answers to the
questions, then the conclusion is inescapable: segregation was pos-
itively correlated with *higher* self-esteem—the opposite of how
the study's results are usually summarized by historians and understood by the general public. (I encourage historians and other
interested parties to double-check my work and/or provide explanations for the mismatch between the public perception of
this study and its actual contents.)

Not only has the Clark study been misexplained by historians, the study's methodology contains at least one flaw that would
probably lead it to be dismissed as junk science were it to be published today: when the study authors switched the order of their
commands, their results changed dramatically. Here is the explanation they give in the study:

Requests 1 through 4 were designed to reveal preferences;
requests 5 through 7 to indicate a knowledge of "racial differences"; and request 8 to show self-identification.

It was found necessary to present the preference requests
first in the experimental situation because in a preliminary
investigation it was clear that the children who had already

identified themselves with the colored doll had a marked tendency to indicate a preference for this doll, and this was not necessarily a genuine expression of actual preference but a reflection of ego involvement. This potential distortion of the data was controlled by merely asking the children to in-dicate their preferences first and then to make identifications with one of the dolls.

To summarize: They did a "preliminary investigation" in which they *first* asked the kids which doll looked like them, and *then* asked which doll was prettier/nicer/etc. And in that prelim-inary investigation, the kids exhibited a preference for the black doll. But rather than take that result at face value and publish it, they switched the question order and got the opposite result.

The Clarks considered it obvious that the initial ordering was "wrong" (meaning the results should be thrown out), whereas the second ordering was "right" (meaning the results should count as solid science). But this is hardly obvious. If the order in which you ask children a series of basic questions totally changes their answers, then you should wonder whether your methodology is sound to begin with. Given how suggestible children are, how mercurial their thoughts and feelings can be, and how sensitive they are to the unspoken expectations of adult authority figures, it is not hard to imagine that their answers might depend on non-verbal cues being given by the adults conducting the study. No-body "preregistered" studies in those days, so they cannot be blamed for the sloppiness of their era. But suffice it to say this would be a major red flag in any study performed today.

In the past eighty years, the doll study has been performed

many times, with varied results. Hraba and Grant (1970) did a study of 160 kids, black and white, and found that most black kids preferred black dolls and most white kids preferred white dolls. Jordan and Hernandez-Reif (2009) completed a study of twenty preschoolers and found that when presented with a range of skin tones, kids had no racial preferences, but when given only two options (black and white), kids chose the self-similar one. Another study (Byrd et. Al., 2016) found that black children did not prefer to play with the white dolls, nor did they say the black doll was ugly or bad. They did, however, say the darkest-skinned doll was "mean."

How much stock should we place in this research? Though I understand why scholars believe these experiments give us reliable knowledge about children's estimation of themselves, the literature contains a fatal methodological flaw. The vast majority of these studies give the child no way of indicating that he or she has no preference. When an adult says, "Show me the prettier doll," the adult is *telling* the child that one doll is in fact prettier—closing the door, in the child's mind, to the possibility that neither doll is prettier. For a child to answer with "no preference" would require the child to disobey the direct instruction of an adult, which small children are trained not to do. Any child with a very slight preference, or no preference at all, is pressured to choose one or the other ("I guess that one?"). In other words, these studies are constructed such that they could not possibly find that children have no racial preferences—even if it were the truth.

Children may even choose the doll that the adult researcher, through nonverbal cues, signals as the "right answer." Many of the researchers who conduct these studies expect to find anti-black racial biases. That is the result that yields the highest status gains in higher education. We know from comparisons between single-blind and double-blind experiments that researchers can influence the result simply by wanting them to turn out a certain way. And this would seem doubly true when the research subjects are suggestible children.

Despite the methodological flaws in this literature, and the varied empirical results, Robin DiAngelo has cited these kinds of studies to make the claim that "white children develop a sense of white superiority as early as preschool." We are all wrong, she claims, when we observe with our own eyes that small kids tend not to care about race and often do not even notice it. In reality, we cannot draw any strong conclusions from research with such flawed methodology and results that have failed to be replicated.

It is one of the great underappreciated mistakes of the Supreme Court that it based its monumental decision to integrate schools on a shoddy experiment with dolls, rather than on the rationale that anti-racist activists had been asking for since abolition—that the government ought to be colorblind.

Neoracists believe that we must indoctrinate children to cure them of racism. I say that children are racially innocent by nature, and we should protect that racial innocence for as long as possible.

APPENDIX D

━━━━━

Broadly, there are two kinds of studies performed to determine whether one thing causes another: observational studies and experimental studies. Observational studies look at real-life data in hindsight and try to control for all confounding variables so as to isolate the effect of one variable upon another. A classic example would be a study that compares drinkers to nondrinkers, controls for every observable variable (e.g., age, gender, race, diet), and then attributes any remaining health disparities to drinking.

These studies have a well-known limitation: there are likely unobservable, immeasurable differences between drinkers and teetotalers. And these confounding variables can never be controlled for. That's why experimental studies are considered the gold standard for proving causation. Because an individual can be randomly assigned to an experimental group or a control group, a potential researcher can cancel out the effects of unobserved, immeasurable variables.

When we have no other choice, we accept observational studies. For instance, babies can't randomly be assigned to a life of drinking or teetotaling. So we must resign ourselves to the lower-confidence conclusions that can be drawn from observational studies. But when it really matters—such as when the FDA must decide whether to approve a drug—we demand randomized, experimental data.

Most ways of studying racism follow the paradigm of observational studies and therefore suffer from the same limitation: researchers can't control for immeasurable variables, like culture, when comparing two racial groups. And there is no reason to think that all immeasurable quantities are randomly distributed. That's why I consider callback studies to be the gold standard for studying racial bias. When we have access to the gold standard in causation research, we should not settle for silver.

There is an interesting variation on the callback experiments that instead use trained actors (one black and one white, say) and send them into identical situations (a job interview or real estate agency, say) to see if they are treated differently. These studies find broadly similar amounts of discrimination against minorities. Even this, however, is not a truly randomized experiment because you cannot control for the subtle differences in behavior, social cues, and overall affectation between two different actors. The two actors are not in fact identical but for their race, whereas two job applications really can be identical but for their race. In this book, I have tried to confine myself to the highest standard of scientific accuracy. So, I have cited the largest meta-analysis of callback studies because I believe it to be the most accurate indicator of the amount of racism in American and Western European societies.

NOTES

INTRODUCTION: WHY WRITE ABOUT RACE?

xv **DiAngelo etiquette outlines:** Robin DiAngelo, *White Fragility: Why It's So Hard for White People to Talk about Racism* (Boston: Beacon Press, 2018), 2, 101, 119, 135.

xvi **To add a cherry:** Ibram X. Kendi, "Pass an Anti-Racist Constitutional Amendment," *Politico*, accessed May 30, 2023, politico.com/interactives /2019/how-to-fix-politics-in-america/inequality/pass-an-anti-racist -constitutional-amendment.

xvi **certain kinds of racial discrimination are good:** Ibram X. Kendi, *How to Be an Anti-Racist* (New York: One World, 2019), 19.

CHAPTER 1: RACE, ANTI-RACISM, AND NEORACISM

5 **The legacy of these genetic differences:** See, for example, David Reich, *Who We Are and How We Got Here* (New York: Pantheon, 2018).

5 **Using standard statistical tools:** Noah A. Rosenberg et al., "Clines, Clusters, and the Effect of Study Design on the Inference of Human Population Structure," *PLoS Genetics* 1, no. 6 (2005): e70, doi.org/10.1371

/journal.pgen.0010070; Jun Z. Li et al., "Worldwide Human Relationships Inferred from Genome-Wide Patterns of Variation," *Science* 319, no. 5866 (2008): 1100–1104, science.org/doi/10.1126/science.1153717.

6 **But it was the Carter administration:** David E. Bernstein, *Classified: The Untold Story of Racial Classification in America* (New York: Bombardier, 2022), 42–44.

6 **someone needs to have one-fourth:** Bernstein, *Classified*, 167.

7 **a specific ethnic group:** Tiffany J. Huang, "The Importance of Asian American Identity for Asian Americans: A Quantitative Analysis," *Data Bits*, a blog for AAPI Data, April 8, 2022, aapidata.com/blog /asian-american-identity.

8 **Christine Combs and Steve Lynn applied:** Bernstein, *Classified*, 10–11.

9 **she was not categorized:** Kao Lee Yang, "I'm Almost Always the Only Hmong American Scientist in the Room. Yet I Was Told I Come from a Group Overrepresented in STEM," *STAT*, November 11, 2021, statnews.com/2021/11/11/only-hmong-scientist-in-the-room-how -overrepresented.

9 **Yet only 9 percent:** Rakesh Kochhar and Anthony Cilluffo, "Income Inequality in the U.S. Is Rising Most Rapidly among Asians," Pew Research Center, July 12, 2018, pewresearch.org/social-trends/2018 /07/12/income-inequality-in-the-u-s-is-rising-most-rapidly-among -asians.

12 **One in five black Americans:** Christine Tamir, "Key Findings about Black Immigrants in the U.S.," Pew Research Center, January 27, 2022, pewresearch.org/fact-tank/2022/01/27/key-findings-about-black -immigrants-in-the-u-s.

13 **"value become sheer sophistical rationalizations":** Jonathan Bean, "Individualists in an Age of Group Discrimination," in *Race and Liberty in America: The Essential Reader*, Jonathan Bean, ed. (Lexington: University Press of Kentucky, 2009), 234.

20 **"I strive to be 'less white'":** Robin DiAngelo, *White Fragility: Why It's So Hard for White People to Talk about Racism* (Boston: Beacon Press, 2018), 150.

21 **stereotypes often do reflect truths:** *Stereotype Accuracy: Towards Appreciating Group Differences*, Yueh-Ting Lee, Lee J. Jussim, and Clark R. McCauley, eds. (Washington, DC: American Psychological Association, 1995).

21 **"Freedom without consequence"**: Ta-Nehisi Coates, "I'm Not Black, I'm Kanye," *The Atlantic*, May 7, 2018, theatlantic.com/entertainment /archive/2018/05/im-not-black-im-kanye/559763.

22 **"then you ain't black"**: Eric Bradner, Sarah Mucha, and Arlette Saenz, "Biden: 'If You Have a Problem Figuring Out Whether You're for Me or Trump, Then You Ain't Black,'" *CNN*, May 22, 2020, cnn .com/2020/05/22/politics/biden-charlamagne-tha-god-you-aint-black /index.html.

23 **"'not his specificity but his fundamentum'"**: Martin Luther King Jr., "Nonviolence and Racial Justice," in *A Testament of Hope: The Essential Writings and Speeches of Martin Luther King Jr.*, James M. Washington, ed. (1986; repr., New York: Harper One, 2003), 6.

23 **Dr. King objected to the term itself**: Martin Luther King Jr., "Stride Towards Freedom," in Washington, ed., *Testament of Hope*, 478.

23 **fictions that people accepted**: Zora Neale Hurston, "Seeing the World as It Is," in *Dust Tracks on a Road* (New York: Harper: 2006).

23 **"Robin DiAngelo, for instance"**: DiAngelo, *White Fragility*, 5, 15.

23 **"Ibram X. Kendi instead argues"**: Ibram X. Kendi, *How to Be an Anti-Racist* (New York: One World, 2019), 35, 201.

24 **white women shouldn't cry**: DiAngelo, *White Fragility*, 131–33.

24 **someone with European ancestry**: Robby Soave, "White-Owned Restaurants Shamed for Serving Ethnic Food: It's Cultural Appropria-tion," *Reason*, May 23, 2105, reason.com/2017/05/23/someone-created -a-list-of-ethnic-restaur; Carolina Moreno, "Portland Burrito Cart Closes After Owners Are Accused of Cultural Appropriation," *Huffington Post*, May 25, 2017, huffpost.com/entry/portland-burrito -cart-closes-after-owners-are-accused-of-cultural-appropriation _n_5926ef7ee4b062f96a348181.

27 **canceling the publication of her novel**: Kat Rosenfield, "The Latest YA Twitter Pile On Forces a Rising Star to Self-Cancel," *Vulture*, January 31, 2019, vulture.com/2019/01/ya-twitter-forces-rising-star -author-to-self-cancel.html; Alexandra Alter, "She Pulled Her Debut Book When Critics Found It Racist. Now She Plans to Publish," *New York Times*, April 29, 2019, nyti.ms/2LqoqUz; Aja Hoggatt, "An Author Canceled Her Own YA Novel over Accusations of Racism. But Is It Really Anti-Black?," *Slate*, January 31, 2019, slate.com/culture/2019/01 /blood-heir-ya-book-twitter-controversy.html; Alexandra Alter; "Y.A.

Author Pulls Her Debut After Pre-Publication Accusations of Racism," *New York Times*, January 31, 2019, nyti.ms/2SlNC0o.

28 **Bell scrambled to clarify:** Isobel Lewis, "Kristen Bell Accused of Glorifying 'Colourblindness' in Children's Book," *Independent*, June 12, 2020, independent.co.uk/arts-entertainment/books/news/kristen-bell-colour-blind-childrens-book-racist-the-world-needs-more-purple-people-a9563211.html.

28 **In a 2019 radio interview:** Bob Kinzel, "He's In for 2020: Bernie Sanders Is Running for President Again," Vermont Public Radio, February 19, 2019, vermontpublic.org/vpr-news/2019-02-19/hes-in-for-2020-bernie-sanders-is-running-for-president-again.

28 **instead of being praised:** Rich Lowry, "The Unbearable Whiteness of Bernie Sanders," *National Review*, February 22, 2019, nationalreview.com/2019/02/bernie-sanders-identity-politics-democratic-party.

28 **he might have held his tongue:** Martin Luther King Jr., *Where Do We Go from Here: Chaos or Community?* (1967; repr., Boston: Beacon Press, 2010), 50.

29 **"Black supremacy is as dangerous":** Martin Luther King Jr., "American Dream" in Washington, ed., *Testament of Hope*, 215.

29 **almost nobody saw the quote as racist:** M. H. Bernstein et al., "Tribalism in American Politics: Are Partisans Guilty of Double-Standards?," *Journal of Open Inquiry in Behavioral Science* (2023), researchers.one/articles/23.02.00006v3.

30 **"pretend that we don't see race":** DiAngelo, *White Fragility*, 40–41.

30 **"a doctrine of the congenital inferiority":** King, *Where Do We Go from Here?*, 49.

30 **In one interview:** Joel D. Aberbach and Jack L. Walker, "The Meanings of Black Power: A Comparison of White and Black Interpretations of a Political Slogan," *American Political Science Review* 64, no. 2 (1970): 367–88, doi.org/10.2307/1953839.

31 **"People of color may also hold prejudices":** DiAngelo, *White Fragility*, 21–22.

33 **a framework based on:** S. T. Fiske, A. J. C. Cuddy, P. Glick, and J. Xu, "A Model of (Often Mixed) Stereotype Content: Competence and Warmth Respectively Follow from Perceived Status and Competition," *Journal of Personality and Social Psychology* 82, no. 6 (2002): 878–902, doi.org/10.1037/0022-3514.82.6.878.

33 **We tend to categorize Thems:** Robert Sapolsky, *Behave: The Biology of Humans at Our Best and Worst* (New York: Penguin, 2017), 411.

34 **opinions that *The Cut* endorsed:** The video was eventually deleted, but has been preserved on other channels. See, for instance, "BLACK People on 'What Are WHITE People Superior At?," posted May 18, 2022, LFR Family, YouTube, youtu.be/UuiA_jRaS8Q.

35 **a key point of contention in the case:** Camille G. Caldera, "Lead Trial Lawyer for SFFA Criticizes Ruling in Harvard Admissions Lawsuit," *Harvard Crimson*, October 9, 2019, thecrimson.com /article/2019/10/9/sffa-lawyer-criticizes-ruling.

35 **55 percent of college students:** M. H. Bernstein and A. L. Bleske-Rechek, "Would People Agree with Hitler When His Statements Are Directed against Whites Instead of Jews?," Presented at the conference of the Society for Open Inquiry in the Behavioral Sciences, Atlanta, GA, February 2023.

37 **The city of Chicago:** "Chicago Automated Speed Enforcement Camera before and after Safety Impact Analysis," City of Chicago, accessed May 30, 2023, chicago.gov/content/dam/city/depts/cdot /CSZ/2023/ASE_Before-After_2019-20_COMBINED_V3.pdf.

38 **When it turned out:** Emily Hopkins and Melissa Sanchez, "Chicago's 'Race-Neutral' Traffic Cameras Ticket Black and Latino Drivers the Most," *ProPublica*, January 11, 2022, propublica.org/article/chicagos -race-neutral-traffic-cameras-ticket-black-and-latino-drivers-the-most.

39 **Consider Ibram X. Kendi's axiom:** "'When I See Racial Disparities, I See Racism,' Discussing Race, Gender and Mobility," *New York Times*, March 27, 2018, nyti.ms/39weQqw.

39 **The white suicide rate in the United States:** "Deaths: Final Data for 2019," *National Vital Statistics Report* 70, no. 8. (2021), 58, cdc.gov/nchs /data/nvsr/nvsr70/nvsr70-08-508.pdf.

40 **A Gallup poll from 2020:** Lydia Saad, "Black Americans Want Police to Retain Local Presence," Gallup, August 5, 2020, news.gallup.com/poll /316571/black-americans-police-retain-local-presence.aspx.

40 **2020 saw the greatest:** John Gramlich, "What We Know about the Increase in U.S. Murders in 2020," Pew Research Center, October 27, 2021, pewresearch.org/fact-tank/2021/10/27/what-we-know-about-the -increase-in-u-s-murders-in-2020.

40 **Minneapolis city council voted to "dismantle":** Dionne Searcey and John Eligon, "Minneapolis Will Dismantle Its Police Force,

Council Members Pledge," *New York Times*, June 7, 2020, nytimes.com
/2020/06/07/us/minneapolis-police-abolish.html.

41 **Later that year, the city council voted:** Liz Navratil, "Minneapolis
Has About 200 Fewer Police Officers Available to Work," *Star Tribune*,
February 4, 2021, startribune.com/minneapolis-has-about-200-fewer
-police-officers-available-to-work/600019034; Holly Bailey, "Minneapolis City Council Votes to Cut Millions from Police Budget amid Record
Crime Rates," *Washington Post*, December 10, 2020, washingtonpost
.com/national-city-council-votes-to-cut-millions-from-police-budget
-amid-record-crime-rates/2020/12/10/af3f14ee-3a8c-11eb-bc68
-96af0daae728_story.html.

41 **Residents successfully sued the city:** Allie Johnson, "Minnesota
Supreme Court Denies Minneapolis' Request to Review Judge's Order
to Hire More Police Officers," *Fox 9 KMSPP*, August 11, 2021, fox9.
com/news/minnesota-supreme-court-denies-minneapolis-request
-to-review-judges-order-to-hire-more-police-officers.

41 **the city council approved:** Liz Navratil, "Minneapolis City Council
Approves $5 Million to Cover Police Overtime," *Star Tribune*, June 17,
2021, startribune.com/minneapolis-city-council-approves
-5-million-to-cover-police-overtime/600069243.

41 **it lost by around 18,000 votes:** "Minneapolis Voters Reject Plan
to Overhaul City Policing," Minneapolis Public Radio News,
November 2, 2021, mprnews.org/story/2021/11/02/minneapolis
-police-ballot-vote.

CHAPTER 2: THE REAL HISTORY OF COLORBLINDNESS

45 **"ink was scarcely dry":** Richard Epstein, *Forbidden Grounds: The Case
against Employment Discrimination Laws* (Cambridge, MA: Harvard
University Press, 1992), 395–96.

46 **Kimberlé Crenshaw, for instance:** *Critical Race Theory: The Key
Writings That Formed the Movement*, Kimberlé Crenshaw, Neil Gotanda,
Gary Peller, and Kendall Thomas, eds. (New York: New Press, 1995), 103.

46 **George Lipsitz, a black-studies professor:** *Seeing Race Again:
Countering Colorblindness across the Disciplines*, Kimberlé Crenshaw,
Luke Charles Harris, Daniel HoSang, and George Lipsitz, eds.
(Oakland: University of California Press, 2019), 24–25.

47 "a government color-blind": *National Anti-slavery Standard*, February 11, 1865, at 1, cols. 1, 6. As quoted in Andrew Kull, *The Color-Blind Constitution* (Cambridge, MA: Harvard University Press, 1992), 61.

48 "NO STATE SHALL MAKE ANY DISTINCTION": *National Anti-Slavery Standard*, July 22, 1865, at 1, col. 2. As quoted in Kull, *Color-Blind Constitution*, 62.

48 "When once the nation": *National Anti-Slavery Standard*, June 8, 1867, at 1, col. 2. As quoted in Kull, *Color-Blind Constitution*, 65.

48 "God has chained this generation": *National Anti-Slavery Standard*, December 28, 1867, at 1, col. 1. As quoted in Kull, *Color-Blind Constitution*, 66.

49 The weaker version: Kull, *Color-Blind Constitution*, 67–87.

49 George Lewis Ruffin: George L. Ruffin, introductory remarks to *A Eulogy on Wendell Phillips: Together with the Proceedings Incident Thereto, Letters, etc.* by Archibald H. Grimké, ed. (Boston, MA: Press of Rockwell and Churchill, 1884), 7.

50 "constitution is color-blind, and neither": Justice John Marshall Harlan, *Plessy v. Ferguson* decision, text available at law.cornell.edu /supremecourt/text/163/537.

51 "Marshall had a 'Bible'": Tinsley E. Yarbrough, *Judicial Enigma: The First Justice Harlan* (New York: Oxford University Press, 1995), 229.

52 Randolph's March on Washington: A. Philip Randolph, "Why Should We March?," from *For Jobs and Freedom: Selected Speeches and Writings of A. Philip Randolph*, A. Philip Randolph, David Lucander, and Andrew Edmund Kersten, eds. (Amherst: University of Massachusetts Press, 2014), 209–10.

52 The Fourteenth Amendment precludes a state: Brown v. Board Brief for Appellants, 1952. naacpldf.org/wp-content/uploads/Oliver -BROWN-Mrs-Richard-Lawton-Mrs-Sadie-Emmanuel-et-al-Appellants -v-BOARD-OF-E-1.pdf.

55 among them celebrated author: Zora Neale Hurston, Letter from Zora Neale Hurston to the *Orlando Sentinel* (1955): Race Mixing. teachingamericanhistory.org/library/index.asp?document=643.

55 Dunbar High, a segregated public school: Thomas Sowell, "Black Excellence: The Case of Dunbar High School," *Public Interest* 35 (Spring 1974): 3–21.

55 **leaving other Jim Crow laws:** Kull, *Color-Blind Constitution*, 151–63.

56 **the language of the bill:** Civil Rights Act of 1964, Title VII, SEC. 2000e-2 (j). Accessed on August 15, 2023, at eeoc.gov/statutes/title-vii -civil-rights-act-1964.

56 **Senator Thomas Kuchel:** Terry Eastland and William J. Bennett, *Counting by Race* (New York: Basic Books, 1979), 206–7.

57 **Senator Hubert Humphrey:** Morris B. Abram, "Racial Quotas: 'Road to Conflict and Tragedies,'" *The New York Times*, July 24, 1983; Steven M. Gillon, *"That's Not What We Meant to Do": Reform and Its Unintended Consequences in Twentieth-Century America* (New York: Norton, 2000), 127.

57 **"only a matter of whose ox is gored":** Alexander Bickel, *The Morality of Consent* (New Haven, CT: Yale University Press, 1975), 133.

58 **Eventually, the Philadelphia Plan:** Melvin Urofsky, *The Affirmative Action Puzzle* (New York: Knopf Doubleday 2020), 92–100.

58 **Clarence Mitchell, the pro-colorblindness:** Urofsky, *Affirmative Action Puzzle*, 93.

58 **one of the lead architects:** Rustin to the editor of *The Wall Street Journal*, March 25, 1974, in Bayard Rustin, *I Must Resist: Bayard Rustin's Life in Letters* (San Francisco: City Light Books, 2012), 395.

59 **A. Philip Randolph's original March:** Randolph, "Why Should We March?," *For Jobs and Freedom*, 209–10.

60 **"the cry 'black power'":** Joel D. Aberbach and Jack L. Walker, "The Meanings of Black Power: A Comparison of White and Black Interpretations of a Political Slogan," *American Political Science Review* 64, no. 2 (1970): 367–88, jstor.org/stable/1953839.

60 **"a reverse Mississippi":** Aberbach and Walker, "Meanings of Black Power," 367.

60 **"a moratorium on inflammatory":** Randolph, *For Jobs and Freedom*, 279–80.

60 **"were explicit in opposing":** Rustin to the editor of *The Wall Street Journal*, in *I Must Resist*, 395.

60 **the hero of the fight:** Quoted in "Mandela Slams 'Reverse Racism,'" *Times Higher Education*, March 24, 1995, timeshighereducation.com /news/mandela-slams-reverse-racism/97135.article.

61 **In 2015, the University of California:** Eugene Volokh, "UC Teaching Faculty Members Not to Criticize Race-Based Affirmative Action,

Call America 'Melting Pot,' and More," *Washington Post*, June 16, 2015, washingtonpost.com/news/volokh-conspiracy/wp/2015/06/16/uc -teaching-faculty-members-not-to-criticize-race-based-affirmative -action-call-america-melting-pot-and-more.

61 **"bound to fail"**: Ibram X. Kendi, *How to Be an Anti-Racist* (New York: One World, 2019), 201.

61 **"I conceive that"**: Frederick Douglass, "God Almighty Made But One Race," his interview with the *Washington Post*, January 26, 1884, in *Race and Liberty in America: The Essential Reader*, Jonathan Bean, ed. (Lexington: University Press of Kentucky, 2009), 98.

62 **"In order to pursue"**: Henry Highland Garnet, *The Past and the Present Condition, and the Destiny, of the Colored Race* (Troy, NY: Steam Press, 1848) 6, archive.org/details/pastpresentcondi00garn/page/n7 /mode/2up.

62 **"blatant denial of the unity"**: Martin Luther King Jr., in *A Testament of Hope: The Essential Writings and Speeches of Martin Luther King Jr.*, James M. Washington, ed. (1986; repr., New York: Harper One, 2003), 478.

62 **"would draw a line of blood distinction"**: Garnet, *Past and Present Condition*, 18–19.

63 **"because I am a man"**: Frederick Douglass, "God Almighty Made But One Race," in Bean, ed., *Race and Liberty* 98.

63 **"My activism did not spring"**: Rustin, "Rustin to Joseph Beam," in *I Must Resist*, 460.

64 **especially toward the end**: Bhaskar Sunkara, "Martin Luther King Was No Prophet of Unity, He Was a Radical," *Guardian*, January 21, 2019, theguardian.com/commentisfree/2019/jan/21/martin-luther -king-jr-day-legacy-radical; Erina Kim-Eubanks, "The Radical Legacy of Dr. King," *Medium*, January 21, 2020, medium.com/firstpres/the -radical-legacy-of-dr-king-in-his-own-words-918c14a3467f; Victoria W. Wolcott, "The Public Has Underestimated the Radicalism of Martin Luther King," *Washington Post*, January 17, 2022, washingtonpost.com /outlook/2022/01/17/public-has-underestimated-radicalism-martin -luther-king-jrs-early-work; Rotimi Adeoye, "Martin Luther King, Jr. Was No Moderate. He Wanted a 'Radical Revolution of Values,'" *Daily Beast*, January 16, 2023, thedailybeast.com/martin-luther-king -jr-was-no-moderate-he-wanted-a-radical-revolution-of-values; Jenn M.

Jackson, "Martin Luther King, Jr. Was a Radical. We Must Reclaim That Legacy," *Al Jazeera*, January 18, 2021, aljazeera.com/features /2021/1/18/martin-luther-king-jr-was-radical-we-must-reclaim-that -legacy.

65 **He even suggests changing the slogan:** Martin Luther King Jr., *Where Do We Go from Here: Chaos or Community?* (1967; repr., Boston: Beacon Press, 2010), 51.

65 **"Let us be dissatisfied until":** Martin Luther King Jr., in Washington, ed., *Testament of Hope*, 251.

65 **"In an effort to achieve":** Martin Luther King Jr., in Washington, ed., *Testament of Hope*, 487.

65 **"God is interested":** Martin Luther King Jr., in Washington, ed., *Testament of Hope*, 215.

65 **"The problem is not a purely racial one":** Martin Luther King Jr., in Washington, ed., *Testament of Hope*, 483.

66 **"The important thing":** Martin Luther King Jr., in Washington, ed., *Testament of Hope*, 6.

66 **"Properly speaking, races do not marry":** Martin Luther King Jr., in Washington, ed., *Testament of Hope*, 478.

66 **"As I stand here":** Martin Luther King Jr., in Washington, ed., *Testament of Hope*, 21.

CHAPTER 3: ELITE NEORACIST INSTITUTIONS

67 **"are white people genetically predisposed":** "Sarah Jeong: NY Times Stands by 'Racist Tweets' Reporter," *BBC*, August 2, 2018, bbc .com/news/world-us-canada-45052534.

69 **Some of them sued:** Michael Levenson, "Judge Blocks $4 Billion U.S. Debt Relief Program for Minority Farmers," *New York Times*, June 23, 2021, nytimes.com/2021/06/23/us/politics/biden-debt-relief-black -farmers.html.

69 **portraying them as angry conservatives:** Jack Healy, "'You Can Feel the Tension': A Windfall for Minority Farmers Divides Rural America," *New York Times*, May 22, 2021, nytimes.com/2021/05/22/us /black-farmers.html.

70 **Approximately 73,000 restaurants closed:** Tim Carman, "How Many Restaurants Closed from the Pandemic? Here's Our Best

Estimate," *Washington Post*, June 21, 2022, washingtonpost.com/food
/2022/06/21/covid-restaurant-closures.

70 **"For the first 21 days":** "SBA Administrator Guzman Announces
Application Opening for $28.6 Billion Restaurant Revitalization
Fund," U.S. Small Business Administration, press release, April 28,
2021, sba.gov/article/2021/apr/27/sba-administrator-guzman-announces
-application-opening-286-billion-restaurant-revitalization-fund.

71 **Around 3,000 restaurant owners:** Stacey Cowley, "How a Relief
Fund for Restaurants Picked Winners and Losers," *New York Times*,
December 24, 2021, nytimes.com/2021/12/24/business/restaurant
-revitalization-fund-problems.html.

71 **According to the SBA:** "SBA Administrator Announces Closure of
Restaurant Revitalization Fund Program," U.S. Small Business
Administration, press release, July 2, 2021, sba.gov/article/2021/jul
/02/sba-administrator-announces-closure-restaurant-revitalization
-fund-program.

71 **only 40 percent of eligible applicants:** "Restaurant Revitalization
Fund: Opportunities Exist to Improve Oversight," U.S. Government
Accountability Office, July 14, 2022, gao.gov/products/gao-22-105442.

72 **recommended that we prioritize:** Yascha Mounk, "Why I'm Losing
Trust in the Institutions," *Persuasion*, December 23, 2020, persuasion
.community/p/why-im-losing-trust-in-the-institutions.

73 **Those guidelines included:** "Covid-19 Oral Antiviral Treatments
Authorized, and Severe Shortage of Oral Antiviral and Monoclonal
Antibody Treatment Products," NY State Department of Health,
December 27, 2021, mssnyenews.org/wp-content/uploads/2021/12
/122821_Notification_107774.pdf.

73 **eight different types of cancer:** *National Vital Statistics Report* 68,
no. 9, U.S. Department of Health and Human Services, June 24, 2019, cdc
.gov/nchs/data/nvsr/nvsr68/nvsr68_09-508.pdf.

73 **More whites were dying of it:** Akilah Johnson and Dan Keating,
"Whites Now More Likely to Die from Covid Than Blacks: Why the
Pandemic Shifted," *Washington Post*, October 19, 2022, washingtonpost
.com/health/2022/10/19/covid-deaths-us-race.

74 **"I had fantasies":** Katie Herzog, "The Psychopathic Problem of the
White Mind," *Free Press*, June 4, 2021, thefp.com/p/the-psychopathic
-problem-of-the-white.

75 **It surveyed 173:** Dion J. Pierre, "Separate but Equal, Again: Neo-Segregation in American Higher Education," National Association of Scholars, April 24, 2019, nas.org/reports/separate-but-equal-again /full-report.

76 **"The persistence of black racial consciousness":** Jared Taylor, "Black Racial Consciousness," *American Renaissance*, October 21, 2011, amren.com/news/2011/10/black_racial_co.

77 **When the college:** Kenneth Clark, "Letter of Resignation from Board of Directors of Antioch College," in *Black Studies: Myths and Realities*, Bayard Rustin, ed. (New York: A. Philip Randolph Educational Fund, 1969), 32.

78 **In July 2021, Texas A&M:** Aaron Sibarium, "Nation's Largest Public University Hit with Class Action Suit over Race-Based Hiring Practices," *Washington Free Beacon*, September 13, 2022, freebeacon .com/campus/nations-largest-public-university-hit-with-class-action -suit-over-race-based-hiring-practices.

79 **Yet according to the new contract:** "Tentative Agreement for the 2021–2023 Teacher Chapter Contract," March 25, 2022, mft59.org/_files /ugd/7a4db8_322ee8a7e471408c92cce0c8e3763d7f.pdf.

79 **The Associated Press wrote:** Associated Press, "Minneapolis Teacher Contract Race Language Ignites Firestorm," *WTOP News*, August 21, 2022, wtop.com/education/2022/08/minneapolis-teacher -contract-race-language-ignites-firestorm.

80 **Instead of these false values:** Susan Edelman, Selim Algar, and Aaron Feis, "Richard Carranza Held 'White-Supremacy Culture' Training for School Admins," *New York Post*, May 20, 2019, nypost .com/2019/05/20/richard-carranza-held-doe-white-supremacy-culture -training.

81 **many Americans are still unaware:** "Police Shootings Database," *Washington Post*, washingtonpost.com/graphics/investigations/police -shootings-database.

81 **I wrote an essay for** *City Journal*: Coleman Hughes, "Stories and Data," *City Journal*, June 14, 2020, city-journal.org/reflections-on-race -riots-and-police.

83 **"32 percent of the unarmed":** *Washington Post*, "Police Shootings Database."

84 **shootings were extremely sexist**: *Washington Post*, "Police Shootings Database."

84 **economist Sendhil Mullainathan:** Sendhil Mullainathan, "Police Killings of Blacks: Here Is What the Data Say," *New York Times*, October 18, 2015, nytimes.com/2015/10/18/upshot/police-killings -of-blacks-what-the-data-says.html; T. R. Miller et al., "Perils of Police Action: A Cautionary Tale from US Data Sets," *Injury Prevention* 23 (2017): 27–32; Roland G. Fryer Jr., "An Empirical Analysis of Racial Differences in Police Use of Force," *Journal of Political Economy* 127, no. 3 (2019): 1210–261.

85 **materials for use in K–12:** Jeff Barrus "Nikole Hannah-Jones Wins Pulitzer Prize for 1619 Project," Pulitzer Center, May 4, 2020, pulitzercenter.org/blog/nikole-hannah-jones-wins-pulitzer-prize-1619 -project.

86 **"more common in the antebellum era":** Leslie M. Harris, "I Helped Fact-Check the 1619 Project. The Times Ignored Me," *Politico,* March 6, 2020, politico.com/news/magazine/2020/03/06/1619-project-new-york -times-mistake-122248.

87 **"Dahomey was dedicated":** Meilan Solly, "The Real Warriors behind 'The Woman King,'" September 15, 2022, *Smithsonian Magazine,* smithsonianmag.com/history/real-warriors-woman-king -dahomey-agojie-amazons-180980750.

88 **choose to wokewash:** "What Matters—Katherine Johnson: NASA Pioneer and 'Computer,'" WHRO Public Media, posted February 25, 2011, YouTube, youtu.be/r8gJqKyIGhE.

CHAPTER 4: WHY NEORACISM IS SPREADING

89 **use of such terms has skyrocketed:** Zach Goldberg, "How the Media Led the Great Racial Awakening," *Tablet*, August 4, 2020, tabletmag.com/sections/news/articles/media-great-racial-awakening.

93 **Support for white supremacy:** The following NYPD chart shows declining police shootings from 1971 to 2010: nyc.gov/html/nypd /downloads/pdf/pr/2010_fdr_preliminary_stats.pdf. *The Los Angeles Times* noted that 2019 marked a thirty-year low in police shootings in Los Angeles: latimes.com/california/newsletter/2021-12-27/los -angeles-police-department-fatal-shootings-by-the-numbers-essential -california.

95 **Michael Brown did not:** "Department of Justice Report Regarding the Criminal Investigation into the Shooting Death of Michael Brown

by Ferguson, Missouri Police Officer Darren Wilson," U.S. Department of Justice, memorandum, March 4, 2015, justice.gov/sites /default/files/opa/press-releases/attachments/2015/03/04/doj_report _on_shooting_of_michael_brown_1.pdf.

98 **"very liberal" Americans:** Eric Kaufmann, "The Social Construction of Racism in the United States," Manhattan Institute, April 2021, media4.manhattan-institute.org/sites/default/files/social-construction -racism-united-states-EK.pdf.

98 **The real number was twelve:** "Police Shootings Database," *Washington Post*, washingtonpost.com/graphics/2019/national/police-shootings-2019.

101 **a sting operation:** Ann Choi, Keith Herbert, Olivia Winslow, and Arthur Browne, "Long Island Divided," *Newsday*, November 17, 2019, projects.newsday.com/long-island/real-estate-agents-investigation /#open-paywall-message.

CHAPTER 5: THE NEORACIST NARRATIVE

105 **"I had no problems whatsoever":** Warren Hughes, *The Birthday Journal*, 30.

108 **"When I see racial disparities":** "'When I See Racial Disparities, I See Racism.' Discussing Race, Gender and Mobility," *New York Times*, March 27, 2018, nyti.ms/39weQqw.

109 **"Americans sitting in prisons":** Ibram X. Kendi, *Stamped from the Beginning* (New York: Bold Type Books, 2016), 1–2.

110 **a fourteen-year age gap:** Katherine Schaeffer, "The Most Common Age among Whites in U.S. Is 58—More Than Double That of Racial and Ethnic Minorities," Pew Research Center, July 30, 2019, pewresearch .org/fact-tank/2016/07/07/biggest-share-of-whites-in-u-s-are-boomers -but-for-minority-groups-its-millennials-or-younger.

110 **same low credit scores:** Andrew Van Dam, "Why the South Has Such Low Credit Scores," *Washington Post*, February 17, 2023, washingtonpost .com/business/2023/02/17/bad-southern-credit-scores.

111 **Orlando Patterson once joked:** Orlando Patterson, "The Social and Cultural Matrix of Black Youth," in *The Cultural Matrix*, Orlando Patterson and Ethan Fosse, eds. (Cambridge, MA: Harvard University Press, 2015), 122.

111 **races were naturally:** Nathan Glazer, *Ethnic Dilemmas* (Cambridge, MA: Harvard University Press, 1983), 218.

112 **Caribbean blacks also earned more:** Van Tran, "More Than Just Race," in *The Cultural Matrix* (Cambridge: Harvard University Press, 2015), 252–80.

112 **Why are approximately 80 percent:** "How China Made the Piano Its Own," *Economist*, December 18, 2019, economist.com/christmas -specials/2019/12/18/how-china-made-the-piano-its-own?fsrc=scn/tw /te/bl/ed/keyboardsoftheworldhowchinamadethepianoitsownchrist masspecials.

113 **the persecuted Japanese minority:** Glazer, *Ethnic Dilemmas*, 59–60.

114 **doughnut shops in California:** Thomas Sowell, *The Quest for Cosmic Justice* (New York: Touchstone, 1999), 36.

114 **the Puerto Rican minority:** Nathan Glazer, *Beyond the Melting Pot* (Cambridge, MA: MIT Press, 1963), 111.

114 **black Caribbeans owned:** Thomas Sowell, *Black Rednecks and White Liberals* (New York: Encounter, 2005), 32.

114 **Jews accounted for half the lawyers:** Sowell, *Black Rednecks and White Liberals*, 84.

114 **black soldiers from northern states:** Sowell, *Black Rednecks and White Liberals*, 23.

114 **Americans raised in Jewish households:** Lisa Keister, "Religion and Wealth: The Role of Religious Affiliation and Participation in Early Adult Asset Accumulation," *Social Forces* 82 (2003): 173–205.

114 **A study of net worth in Boston:** Ana Patricia Muñoz, et al., "The Color of Wealth in Boston," Duke University, The New School, and Federal Reserve Bank of Boston, March 25, 2015, bostonfed.org /publications/one-time-pubs/color-of-wealth.aspx.

117 **South Asians were 30 percent:** Louis Lippens, Siel Vermeiren, and Stijn Baert, "The State of Hiring Discrimination: A Meta-Analysis of (Almost) All Recent Correspondence Experiments" (discussion paper no. 14966, Institute of Labor Economics, Bonn, Germany, 2022), dx.doi .org/10.2139/ssrn.4114491.

117 **Chinese Americans earn $1.18:** Per capita income calculated from data from the US Census and the American Community Survey.

119 **"Errors are deadly":** "Air-Traffic Controllers Are Vetted and Competent," *Wall Street Journal*, June 21, 2018, wsj.com/articles/air-traffic -controllers-are-vetted-and-competent-1529592742.

119 **A class action suit:** Jason Riley, "Affirmative Action Lands in the Air Traffic Control Tower," Manhattan Institute, June 3, 2015, manhattan

-institute.org/html/affirmative-action-lands-air-traffic-control-tower
-6226.html.

120 **"The only remedy to present discrimination":** Ibram X. Kendi,
How to Be an Anti-Racist (New York: One World, 2019), 19.

121 **forced to cut their braids:** Edward J. M. Rhoads, *Manchus and Han:
Ethnic Relations and Political Power in Late Qing and Early Republican
China, 1861–1928* (Seattle: University of Washington Press, 2000).

124 **"they are worse off":** Michelle Alexander, *The New Jim Crow: Mass
Incarceration in the Age of Colorblindness* (New York: New Press, 2010),
228.

125 **in 2021 it was at 94 percent:** Justin McCarthy, "U.S. Approval of
Interracial Marriage at New High of 94%," Gallup, September 10,
2021, news.gallup.com/poll/354638/approval-interracial-marriage
-new-high.aspx.

125 **By 2021 that number reached 57:** Kim Parker and Amanda Barroso,
"In Vice President Kamala Harris, We Can See How America Has
Changed," Pew Research Center, February 25, 2021, pewresearch.org
/fact-tank/2021/02/25/in-vice-president-kamala-harris-we-can-see
-how-america-has-changed.

125 **in 2019 it stood at 96 percent:** Jeffrey M. Jones, "Some Americans
Reluctant to Vote for Mormon, 72-Year-Old Presidential Candidates,"
Gallup, February 20, 2007, news.gallup.com/poll/26611/some-americans
-reluctant-vote-mormon-72yearold-presidential-candidates.aspx; Justin
McCarthy, "Less Than Half in U.S. Would Vote for a Socialist for
President," Gallup, May 9, 2019, news.gallup.com/poll/254120/less-half
-vote-socialist-president.aspx.

125 **the national incarceration rate:** U.S. Department of Justice statistics
for 2001: bjs.ojp.gov/content/pub/pdf/p01.pdf; U.S. Department of
Justice statistics for 2017: bjs.ojp.gov/content/pub/pdf/p17.pdf.

125 **the black teenage birth rate:** Centers for Disease Control birth data
for 2002: cdc.gov/nchs/data/nvsr/nvsr52/nvsr52_10.pdf; Centers for
Disease Control birth data for 2017: cdc.gov/nchs/data/nvsr/nvsr67
/nvsr67_08-508.pdf.

126 **blacks at every level:** "Report on the Economic Well-Being of U.S.
Households in 2018," U.S. Federal Reserve System, May 2019, federal-
reserve.gov/publications/files/2018-report-economic-well-being
-us-households-201905.pdf.

126 **black girls and white girls:** Chetty et al., "Race and Economic Opportunity in the United States: An Intergenerational Perspective," *Quarterly Journal of Economics* 135, no. 2 (2020): 711–83.

126 **began living socially as white:** Ricardo Dahis, Emily Nix, and Nancy Qian, "Choosing Racial Identity in the United States, 1880–1940," (working paper no. 26465, National Bureau of Economic Research, Cambridge, MA, 2019), 10.3386/w26465.

127 **They found the opposite trend:** F. Antman and B. Duncan, "Incentives to Identify: Racial Identity in the Age of Affirmative Action," *Review of Economics and Statistics* 97, no. 3 (2015): 710–13, 10.1162 /REST_a_00527.

128 **The counterprotesters didn't:** Elaine Godfrey and Madeleine Carlisle, "'Unite the Right' Fizzles amid a Boisterous Counterprotest," *Atlantic*, August 12, 2018, theatlantic.com/politics/archive/2018/08 /unite-the-right-fizzles-amid-a-boisterous-counter-protes/567374.

128 **the Ku Klux Klan had:** *Tattered Robes: The State of the Ku Klux Klan in the United States*, Anti-Defamation League, 2016, web.archive.org /web/20171118095816/adl.org/sites/default/files/documents/assets/pdf /combating-hate/tattered-robes-state-of-kkk-2016.pdf; Cindy Alexander, "Statistics: Immigration in America, Ku Klux Klan Membership: 1915–1940s," Gilder Lehrman Institute of American History, accessed May 31, 2023, gilderlehrman.org/history-resources/teaching-resource /statistics-immigration-america-ku-klux-klan-membership-1840-1940.

128 **the Flat Earth Society:** Douglas Martin, "Charles Johnson, 76, Proponent of Flat Earth," *New York Times*, March 25, 2001, nytimes.com/2001 /03/25/us/charles-johnson-76-proponent-of-flat-earth.html.

130 **The US House of Representatives formally apologized:** "Congress Apologizes for Slavery, Jim Crow," NPR, July 30, 2008, npr.org/2008 /07/30/93059465/congress-apologizes-for-slavery-jim-crow; Frank James, "Senate Apologizes for Slavery and Jim Crow," NPR, June 18, 2009, npr.org/sections/I-way/2009/06/senate_apologizes_for_slavery .html.

130 **eight other states have followed suit:** Michelle Hackman, "Delaware Just Became the 9th State to Apologize for Slavery," *Vox*, February 11, 2016, vox.com/2016/2/11/10965548/delaware-slavery.

131 **the exhibit on slavery:** Peggy McGlone, "Crowds at African American Museum Are Expected to Get Even Bigger," *Washington Post*, March 23,

2017, washingtonpost.com/entertainment/museums/crowds-at
-african-american-museum-are-expected-to-get-even-bigger/2017/03
/23/7719d3d8-0e58-11e7-ab07-07d9f521f6b5_story.html.

131 "compensatory justice": Melvin I. Urofsky, *Affirmative Action Puzzle:
A Living History from Reconstruction to Today* (New York: Knopf
Doubleday, 2020), 95.

132 More Americans watched *Roots*: Josef Adalian, "Roots Is Still One of
the Biggest TV Success Stories Ever," *Vulture*, May 26, 2016, vulture
.com/2016/05/roots-miniseries-ratings-were-off-the-charts.html.

132 NBC News, for instance: Mark Medish and Daniel Lucich, "Congress Must Officially Apologize for Slavery before America Can Think
about Reparations," NBC News, August 30, 2019, nbcnews.com/think
/opinion/congress-must-officially-apologize-slavery-america-can-think
-about-reparations-ncna1047561.

133 fierce resistance to soul-searching: "Make Juneteenth a National
Holiday for the American Dream of Liberty and Justice for All," *USA
Today*, July 8, 2020, usatoday.com/story/opinion/todaysdebate/2020
/07/08/why-juneteenth-should-national-holiday-all-americans-
editorials-debate/5385438002.

133 Arabs enslaved as many as: Ronald Segal, *Islam's Black Slaves: The Other
Black Diaspora* (New York: Farrar, Straus and Giroux, 2001), 56–57.

133 a common colloquial word: "Viewpoint from Sudan—Where Black
People Are Called Slaves," BBC, July 26, 2020, bbc.com/news
/world-africa-53147864; Theola Labbe, "A Legacy Hidden in Plain
Sight," *Washington Post*, January 11, 2004, washingtonpost.com
/archive/politics/2004/01/11/a-legacy-hidden-in-plain-sight.

136 "The research in epigenetics": Benedict Carey, "Can We Really
Inherit Trauma?" *New York Times*, December 10, 2018, nytimes.com
/2018/12/10/health/mind-epigenetics-genes.html.

137 "there is no group of people": Orlando Patterson, *Slavery and Social
Death: A Comparative Study* (Cambridge, MA: Harvard University
Press, 2018), xxvii.

137 "there is no known slaveholding society": Patterson, *Slavery and
Social Death*, 4.

138 outbreaks of hiccups: Helen Lewis, "The Twitching Generation,"
Atlantic, February 27, 2022, theatlantic.com/ideas/archive/2022
/02/social-media-illness-teen-girls/622916; Robert Bartholomew, "The
School That Caught the Hiccups," *Psychology Today*, June 27, 2016,

psychologytoday.com/us/blog/its-catching/201606/the-school-caught
-the-hiccups.

141 **"if you are white"**: Robin DiAngelo, *White Fragility: Why It's So Hard for White People to Talk about Racism* (Boston: Beacon Press, 2018), 7.

144 **Thomas Sowell is black:** The *London School of Economics and Political Science's blog, Review of Books* amended the review in November 2017 and appended this comment: "The original post contained the line 'easy for a rich white man to say.' This has been removed and we apologise for the error." Later still, the entire review was removed from the *LSE's Review of Books* website. In its place, the editors posted the following: "This book review of Thomas Sowell's Intellectuals and Society, originally published in 2012, has been removed. The original review included the line 'easy for a rich white man to say' in reference to the book's author, Thomas Sowell. This was a factually inaccurate and offensive error. The error was removed and an amendment added to the post in 2017. A subsequent review of the post in 2020 has determined that the book review did not meet the minimum standard for publication and has consequently been removed. We deeply apologise for the error": Editors , "Book Review: Intellectuals and Society by Thomas Sowell," London School of Economics and Political Science, *Review of Books*, May 26, 2012, blogs.lse.ac.uk /lsereviewofbooks/2012/05/26/book-review-intellectuals-and -society-by-thomas-sowell.

146 **white people should never cry:** DiAngelo, *White Fragility*, 131–33.

146 **attributes of "white dominant culture":** Peggy McGlone, "African American Museum Site Removes 'Whiteness' Chart After Criticism from Trump Jr. and Conservative Media," *Washington Post*, July 17, 2020, washingtonpost.com/entertainment/museums/african-american -museum-site-removes-whiteness-chart-after-criticism-from-trump -jr-and-conservative-media/2020/07/17/4ef6e6f2-c831-11ea-8ffe -372be8d82298_story.html.

146 **A similar book, *Dismantling Racism*:** Susan Edelman, Selim Algar, and Aaron Feis, "Richard Carranza Held 'White-Supremacy Culture' Training for School Admins," *New York Post*, May 20, 2019, nypost .com/2019/05/20/richard-carranza-held-doe-white-supremacy-culture -training.

149 **some Mormons were privately offended:** Jenny Kleeman, "What Do Mormons Think about 'The Book of Mormon'?," *Vice*, March 21,

2013, vice.com/en/article/vdn9z4/i-asked-some-mormons-what-they
-thought-about-the-book-of-mormon; Chris Campbell, "Mormons
React to 'The Book of Mormon' Musical Coming to Salt Lake City,"
Utah Public Radio, July 30, 2015, upr.org/utah-news/2015-07-30
/mormons-react-to-the-book-of-mormon-musical-coming-to-salt
-lake-city.

149 **The *Book of Mormon*'s portrayal:** Michael Paulson, "As Broadway
returns, Shows Rethink and Restage Depictions of Race," *New York
Times,* October 23, 2021, nytimes.com/2021/10/23/theater/broadway
-race-depictions.html.

149 **NBC News ran an op-ed:** Brennan Nevada Johnson, "Hey Chris
Rock, I'm a Bald Black Woman—and It's Not a Joke," *NBC News,*
March 28, 2022, nbcnews.com/think/opinion/chris-rock-s-joke-about
-jada-pinkett-smith-was-rooted-ncna1293481.

149 ***USA Today* ran a piece:** Sara M. Moniuszko, "Jada Pinkett Smith,
Chris Rock and Why His Hair Joke Was So Problematic," *USA Today,*
March 28, 2022, usatoday.com/story/life/health-wellness/2022/03
/28/chris-rock-jada-pinkett-smith-oscars-joke-black-women-hair
/7190552001.

149 **Meanwhile, the same week:** *The Problem with Jon Stewart,* season 1,
episode 8, "Racism," directed by Andre Allen, written by Kristen
Acimovic, Henrik Blix, and Rob Christensen, aired March 24, 2022, on
Apple TV, tv.apple.com/us/episode/racism/umc.cmc.2pdsx0nj6zh6lx
57hho4w5ffp?action=play.

150 **The top 10 percent:** "Distribution of Household Wealth in the
U.S. Since 1989," U.S. Federal Reserve System, last updated June 16,
2023, federalreserve.gov/releases/z1/dataviz/dfa/distribute/table
/#quarter:129;series:Net%20worth;demographic:networth;population:
all;units:shares.

CHAPTER 6: SOLVING THE PROBLEM OF RACISM IN AMERICA

159 **racially- and gender-coded names:** Katherine L. Milkman,
Modupe Akinola, and Dolly Chugh, "What Happens Before? A Field
Experiment Exploring How Pay and Representation Differentially
Shape Bias on the Pathway into Organizations," *Journal of Applied
Psychology* 100, no. 6 (2015): 1678–1712, doi.org/10.1037/apl0000022.

160 "If Black people make up": Ibram X. Kendi, *Stamped from the Beginning* (New York: Bold Type Books, 2017), 1–2.

163 "If the applicant": Melvin I. Urofsky, *The Affirmative Action Puzzle* (New York: Knopf Doubleday, 2020), 191.

164 Pew asked 6,637 American adults: Nikki Graf, "Most Americans Say Colleges Should Not Consider Race or Ethnicity in Admissions," Pew Research Center, February 25, 2019, pewresearch.org/fact-tank/2019 /02/25/most-americans-say-colleges-should-not-consider-race-or -ethnicity-in-admissions.

164 Gallup asked 6,502 American adults: Jim Norman, "Americans' Support for Affirmative Action Programs Rises," Gallup, February 27, 2019, news.gallup.com/poll/247046/americans-support-affirmative -action-programs-rises.aspx.

166 "I just read a blk girl": *Students for Fair Admissions Inc. v. University of North Carolina, et al.*, "Petition for a Writ of Certiorari Before Judgment to the United States Court of Appeals for the Fourth Circuit," (case no. 14-cv-954-LCB, November 11, 2021), supremecourt.gov/DocketPDF /21/21-707/199684/20211111164129792_UNC%20Cert%20Petition %20-%20Nov%2011%20-%20330pm%20002.pdf, 5–6.

166 Asians and whites had to score: See chapter three in Thomas J. Espenshade and Alexandria Walton Radford, *No Longer Separate, Not Yet Equal: Race and Class in Elite College Admission and Campus Life* (Princeton, NJ: Princeton University Press, 2014).

167 less than 5 percent: Raj Chetty et al., "Mobility Report Cards: The Role of Colleges in Intergenerational Mobility" (working paper no. 23618, National Bureau of Economic Research, Cambridge, MA, 2017), nber.org/system/files/working_papers/w23618/w23618.pdf.

167 disproportionately high percentage: Sara Rimer and Karen W. Arenson, "Top Colleges Take More Blacks, but Which Ones?," *New York Times*, June 24, 2004, nytimes.com/2004/06/24/us/top-colleges -take-more-blacks-but-which-ones.html.

167 Princeton sociologist Thomas Espenshade estimates: Thomas Espenshade, "Moving Beyond Affirmative Action," *New York Times*, October 4, 2012, nytimes.com/2012/10/05/opinion/moving-beyond -affirmative-action.html.

168 data from eight elite colleges: Espenshade, "Moving Beyond Affirmative Action."

170 **higher attrition rate:** P. Arcidiacono, E. M. Aucejo, and K. Spenner, "What Happens after Enrollment? An Analysis of the Time Path of Racial Differences in GPA and Major Choice," *IZA Journal of Labor Economics* 1, no. 5 (2012), 1–24, doi.org/10.1186/2193-8997-1-5.

171 **add more people of color:** Mamta Badkar and Andrew Edgecliffe-Johnson, "US Boardrooms Fail to Reflect Country's Demographics," *Financial Times*, June 12, 2020, ft.com/content/c47c9b63-26c0-4487-94a9-4db7da585fbd.

171 **The state of California:** Jeanne Sahadi, "California Will Now Require More Diversity on Company Boards," CNN, September 30, 2020, cnn.com/2020/09/30/success/board-diversity-california-law/index.html.

171 **double the number:** Satya Nadella, "Addressing Racial Injustice," *Microsoft Corporate Blogs*, June 23, 2020, blogs.microsoft.com/blog/2020/06/23/addressing-racial-injustice.

171 **racial diversity quota:** Soraya Nadia McDonald, "CBS Announces New Goals for Diversity in Network Writers' Rooms," Andscape, July 13, 2020, andscape.com/features/cbs-announces-new-goals-for-diversity-in-network-writers-rooms.

173 **"Higher education has a responsibility":** Espenshade, "Moving Beyond Affirmative Action."

173 **After studying thirty-nine charter schools:** Will Dobbie and Roland G. Fryer Jr., "Getting Beneath the Veil of Effective Schools: Evidence from New York City," *American Economic Journal: Applied Economics* 5, no. 4 (2013): 28–60.

174 **The overall result:** Roland G. Fryer Jr., "Injecting Charter School Best Practices into Traditional Public Schools: Evidence from Field Experiments," *Quarterly Journal of Economics* 129, no. 3 (2014): 1355–1407, doi.org/10.1093/qje/qju011.

APPENDIX A

184 **genome clusters can be measured:** See Noah A. Rosenberg et al., "Clines, Clusters, and the Effect of Study Design on the Inference of Human Population Structure," *PLoS Genetics* 1, no. 16 (2005): e70, doi.org/10.1371/journal.pgen.0010070; Jun Z. Li et al., "Worldwide Human Relationships Inferred from Genome-Wide Patterns of

Variation," *Science* 319, no. 5866 (2008): 1100–1104, science.org/doi/
10.1126/science.1153717.

187 **human beings are born:** Leonard Sax, "How Common Is Intersex? A
Response to Anne Fausto-Sterling," *Journal of Sex Research* 39, no. 3
(2002): 174–78, doi.org/10.1080/00224490209552139.

APPENDIX B

189 **"we are not there yet":** Stokely Carmichael and Charles V. Hamilton,
Black Power: The Politics of Liberation in America (New York: Vintage
Books, 1992), 54; Patricia J. Williams, *Seeing a Color-Blind Future: The
Paradox of Race* (New York: Noonday Press, 1998), 4.

APPENDIX C

196 **Hraba and Grant:** J. Hraba and G. Grant, "Black Is Beautiful: A
Reexamination of Racial Preference and Identification," *Journal of
Personality and Social Psychology* 16, no. 3 (1970): 398–402, doi.org
/10.1037/h0030043.

196 **Jordan and Hernandez-Reif:** P. Jordan and M. Hernandez-Reif,
"Reexamination of Young Children's Racial Attitudes and Skin Tone
Preferences," *Journal of Black Psychology* 35 (2009): 388–403, doi.org
/10.1177/0095798409333621.

197 **"white children develop":** Robin DiAngelo, *White Fragility: Why It's
So Hard for White People to Talk about Racism* (Boston: Beacon Press), 47.

INDEX